Troubled Joy

Troubled Joy

Lincolnshire Psalms

Derek Webster

Published in
Great Britain in 2003 by
Kenelm Press
60 Queen's Parade
Cleethorpes
Lincolnshire DN35 0DG

ISBN 0 9526230 3 X

Cover design by Chris Webster

Printed and bound by
Robert Melton
Grimsby Copy Centre
Grimsby DN31 3BH

Introduction

The psalms stand very close to the heart of Christian prayer and worship. From the earliest times, the church has seen in them a means by which God draws near to his people. The shadow of Jesus of Nazareth lies across them and the Holy Spirit breathes within them. Because they are God's word, the church has used them in public and private worship since the time of the apostles. This continues the tradition of the first psalmists in ancient Israel, going back at least to King David and possibly earlier. They form a book of prayer and praise. Originally written in Hebrew and intended for Israel's worship at particular times, they speak to men and women in all times. Their motifs are universal, their moods and fears, joys and hopes, agonies and delights go beyond any local significance. Chiming with the experiences of people everywhere, they express a deep longing for God and a joy when he answers and the dialogue of love begins.

Troubled Joy attempts to re-imagine the original Psalter for a new time, to re-present for the beginning of this century the youthful strength of a unique collection of songs which explores the depths of God's relationship with his peoples. As a re-creation, a re-imagining rather than a translation, as an evocation rather than a paraphrase, it does not mirror every verse of the psalms in English or parallel each phrase and thought, each picture and metaphor. Instead, it responds to the spirit of the text very freely. While attempting to be faithful to the spirituality and poetry, to the audacity and energy of the words of the original, it tries to place this world within their truth. It does not mimic the style or use the forms and technical apparatus of Hebrew poetry. And it disregards many of the conventions common to translators, for this is a Psalter that seeks to draw not to scholarly analysis but to prayer. As does the Hebrew Psalter.

Yet those who approach it for the first time can easily become dispirited. There are many obscurities. Places and people are strange. Ideas and assumptions are puzzling. Historical, religious and cultural backgrounds are unfamiliar because each language, each culture, constructs and interprets its own world in a unique way. To resolve these issues is to slip from prayer and worship into academic study. And that is not necessary. Though the lives of modern men and women are set at a great distance from those for whom the original Psalter was written, this remoteness is liberating. It can free them from the external authority of the text, give them the opportunity to sing with fresh vigour and respond to God in contemporary ways. It can refresh a Christian understanding of the Psalter.

Each generation has its poets who offer this understanding. Inspired by the Psalter, they have responded to it in imaginative and highly individual ways. John Milton and William Cowper, Henry Vaughan and Christopher Smart, Francis Bacon and Miles Coverdale, with many others, are among those who have walked closely with King David and his musicians. In more recent times, so have Peter Levi and Ronald Knox, Eugene Peterson and Gordon Jackson.

It is not with any idea of replacing their work that *Troubled Joy* is written. Their visions have an authenticity and truth, an energy and cadence that no one would wish to change. Indeed, Miles Coverdale's Psalter remains one of the glories of Christian spirituality. Rather, this Psalter is written in a spirit of fidelity to Coverdale's vision that men and women should be encouraged to embed themselves in the adoration proposed by the psalms. It is a homage to those poets whose gifts have helped men and women in earlier times to hone their lives on these songs and sing them for themselves.

The psalmists, known and unknown, are called and moved by God. They weep and wait for him, argue and agonise before him, adore and delight in him. *Troubled Joy* seeks to respond to the beauty and power of their ancient prayers with a modern writing that brings them into the present. Its effort is to locate what is often difficult to distil in exact translation. If these re-creations make readers curious about the original and send them back to reflect on their own lives within the context of the Psalter and nourishing prayer, then their job is doubly done.

The subtitle, Lincolnshire Psalms, expresses my affection for the people of that county. In its villages and towns, among its rural communities and seaside places, and above all in the city and Cathedral of Lincoln, reflection for this writing took place.

It is a pleasure to thank friends and colleagues who have helped in the writing of this book. Mike Bottery and John Smith of Hull University, Patricia Batstone, Geoffrey Daniel, as well as Bishop John Brown and members of the congregation of St. Peter's Church, Cleethorpes, have given valued encouragement. As with Chris Webster, Henry Tickner's practical help has enhanced its design. Wendy, my wife, has been a constant inspiration and shown deep understanding during long hours at the computer. Grateful thanks go to my Salvation Army friend, Envoy Molly Tickner, with whom the text was discussed and whose advice was especially valuable. Without her constant support, eagle eye and common sense, *Troubled Joy* would not have reached publication. Her support is particularly appreciated for it was given when her own life had many other commitments and pressures.

Troubled Joy is dedicated to Iris Webster and Henry Montgomery, both born this year. I hope that one day they will understand for themselves why grandpa had to write a book of psalms.

Hull University
2003

Contents

Book Two

Book Three

Book Four

Book Five

Book
One

1   Good and Evil

A black tree infiltrates
A stale ditch.
Its smug thorns pin those who
    nest in confusion,
    twitter in cliques,
    annex life.

They lose truth,
Clutch the least,
Molest reason; for they
    inhabit marred passions,
    father freedom's evil,
    obliterate grace.

But to the drum of the sun,
A young tree's slow ascent
Seeks a holy heart,
    fresh with infant joy,
    brimming life,
    and love's courtesy.

A holy bench. The Lord sets
Wine and hopes answered,
Gives guests the eyes
    to know the throb of
    eternity in the quiet
    ticking of shed days.

Two trees, two ways:
One sunless set in night,
One transfixed beyond light.

Full darkness swathes the earth;
Intrepid goodness is evil's disguise.
Few know truth: none love it.

Powerful men conceal
Treachery with smiling lies.
In this alley, truth is a beggar.

But God mocks empires of futility
And speaks. *In the place of my presence*
A king is crowned: his name is truth.

From love he comes, with love he lodges.
His gift is the nations. In love he will rule them,
Losing bonds: checking the unjust.

Listen deeply, unpick indifference and
Recover light, for God is gracious to
Those who seek a love that does not rust.

3   My Shield

Lies swarm over me: hate stares me out.
Gravediggers taunt, *God is silent!*

My scream: inaudible. From distant winds
You call, *I am your shield forever.*

In darkness tongues shame, fists bruise;
Yet you stand with me, turn this anger.

Awakening to a sun baptising light, I know –
In day and sleep – your shadow shelters me.

It shows this: the key past death
Is dedication and obedience to you.

4 A Night Dialogue

From a narrow ravine – trapped fast – you
Led me to sunlit uplands. You are the God
Who hears those seeking grace. You say,

The dryness of lies and scorpion slander
Have defiled my spirit and made you a people
Loathsome to me.

Always you come to faithful servants.
With opening arms, you gift love
To those you save. You say,

Scrap flittering trappings of unreality;
Tear away pretence from living;
Ponder in quietness.

Despondent, I urge, "Act for me."
Then I know I shall awake in the
Joy of your presence, overarching.

5   A Prayer for Guidance

Lord, though thoughts stumble,
Tumble into words,
Know the agony of my spirit.

Hear the plea of my rough heart.
Take the sacrifice I make of your
Fluent days in my dispersed life.

Your holiness shuns the squalid lies
Of trickster tongues and deceitful kin,
Who barter for justice, defile living.

In slanting shafts of sun, I attend to
The temple of your morning presence,
Murmuring adoration, asking guidance.

My way is in disarray, beset by
Fawning enemies feigning truth.
Turn them: unmask my path,

For you delight in those who seek you.
Your presence dwells with them:
Love transfiguring life.

Hunched in dread, I stare to the floor
Deserving censure.
Awe-full God, temper fury with mercy.

Stooped in melancholy, racked with pain,
I hear cynics whisper.
Absent God, will you come?

Lean down, touch my heart.
How will I sing your songs if I perish,
If death drains me out?

Bend to me. My flesh is seared,
My eyes are puffed and red-sore with
Weeping, anguish withers my heart.

Rise high. Look to the light;
Villainous clouds scatter.
The Lord's sun-glow glory will enfold me.

7 A Petition

My God, shelter me, for anguish is my prayer.
As lions track and rip apart their prey,
So darkness trails and traps me in its snare.

My God, shelter me, for I am innocent.
Only if I have seduced good and saved evil,
Shall night drag me to its torment.

My God, judge me, see my trials,
Before gathered peoples, ascend your throne.
Establish my integrity, wipe out what defiles.

My God, raise your arm, shield me with love.
I have no wit for knowledge, yet I seek you.
Quell my heart, pour out its cure from above.

In shadows, disturbing icons entice.
Break them with the rage of justice,
Draw them to the darks they devised.

Spilling words, wandering thoughts, throng.
Stoop down now. For you, love's greatest
God, I sing my song.

8 Creator and Creation

Majestic creator:

You paint in splendour over the skies,
    rainbows and clouds across a lemon sun.
You set for play, spinning galaxies
    and ox-eye daisies in squelchy ooze.

The fire of your wonders is awesome
    and stills your foes. You overthrow their lore
by the choral chortle of little ones,
    clapping and babbling songs for you.

I ponder starflowers strewn in secret
    across profound heavens, a bleached moon,
and sorrel in the hedgerow: astonished
    that you call to us, cherish us.

But you do, and the shadow of what is illimitable
    woos. Imaged in love, crowned with freedom,
you charge us to watch over your creation,
    fresh-fingered, stained with beauty.

Watch over creatures who tread far meadows,
    sea monsters who take unseen paths
In the ocean's deep, birds who fly on airy tracks.
    With us they are enfolded in fiery silence:

Majestic creator.

9   Praise Our Judge

Sea grass is fullness further than thought;
Red crabs are a manifold, unrecognised.
Your gifts, Lord, outdo sight, outrun dreams;
All I am shouts, *Amazing King!*

Enthroned, you justify my days to foes who
Melt away before your dazzling presence.
You condemn evil; those who trade in it fall
To dust and leave no name in their cities.

From dawn to the close of time, you
Judge with fairness, giving proper dues.
Those who are crushed and brutally used
Keep faith, for you never desert them.

We hymn you with a heart that is yours.
Though enemies pursue to the edge,
To the gorge where death rises, your love
Leans down, captures me for yourself.

The subterfuge of those who use night
Rebounds. They thrash in pits dredged
For their own prey, are tangled in threads –
Spun from deceits – secretly set for me.

Retribution: God comes! He redeems his poor,
Shows the rebellious the frailty of bones, the
Brief span of each life. These are forgotten,
Like dry grass scorched in a wind of fire.

10 Where Are You?

Because you are hidden
In the seasons of the night,
Further than the limits of thought,
By a subtle calculus of illusion, men conclude,
He has gone.

Because you are hidden,
Eyeless, they abuse, use violence.
Protected by your absence,
Their savagery seeps through time,
A creed without roots.

Because you are hidden,
They defy, beguile and leer,
Driving venal desire without
Restraint, scholars in an
Archaeology of evil.

Because you are hidden,
They circle in shadows and harry the good.
Justice is skewered to the haggard earth,
Its only requiem their boast,
All's well with us and ours.

Because you are hidden,
They ambush the poor. Like lions with prey,
They suck death's bones. *There is no law,*
They say – and secretly add,
He is dead.

You outlast the conjuring words
Of those who dismiss you,
But answer all who call to you.
Their shapeless sorrow
Remains your shadow.

Rise up! Reveal yourself,
A selfless light, in whose hope
Faltering exiles resume the road
Towards joy – nailed to love –
And a new, cock-crowing, homecoming.

11 My Refuge

The Lord shelters me:
My heart is in his safekeeping.
Yet friends – who are not
Friends – warn me, saying,

Quickly, like a sparrow returning
*   to her nest,*
*   go to the hills;*
Vicious men have tracked you down,
*   bent bows, strung arrows,*
*   sighted their target: your heart!*
When the bedrock of law and
*   custom is split, any honest person*
*   is exposed.*

I tell them that the Lord,
    whose throne is on the rainbow,
    makes a dwelling in my heart.

He watches those who defy him,
    aware of their
    craving and passions.

When the earth quakes, they will
    scream unheard in burning winds;
    ancient seas of fire will engulf them.

Only those who love
    the Lord delight
    in his presence.

12 Falsehood and Truth

These fakes, spit out truth,
Rinse their mouths with lies,
Embargo those who love you, Lord.

These seducers, allegorise truth,
Scour out honesty and fidelity,
Swindle people with shy talk.

These fixers – without principle –
Separate truth from living, say,
We are in control.

But you, the Lord, speak.
I will see the plight of my people.
I will hear the sobbing of my children.
I will bring them to a green haven.

Opportunists, who strut many days,
Exalting odious compromise,
Leaving truth untenanted,

Forget that you guard us.
Your word is whitest light;
Your promise, dazzling suns.

13 Waiting

Lord, will you always
Turn away from me?
Shun me?
Abandon me to pain?
Annul mercy?
Deliver me without pity
To my enemies?

Lord, my heart waits for your love.
Answer it with the beauty of
Your presence
Before brooding death smothers
My soul
And those who harry me
Shout, *Victory!*

Surely those who hate me
Will not see me fall.
Your strength
Is a redeeming circle,
Shielding me.
Waiting at your borders, I ponder
Ways of love.

14 Cynics

Smart cynics dismiss his shadow – an irrelevance.
In denial dwells evasion, escape from duty,
Hostility to virtue.

But God is with his people – illimitable love.
He weeps. Not one seeks him, not one
Lives for goodness.

People no longer understand words – *holy, God.*
They sponsor evil and, without conscience,
Ply sad plausibility.

Yet, unknowing, they stand in light – his grace.
He thwarts their schemes and reaches out to
His beloved ones.

He draws those who seek him – a remnant.
In times to be, he will be again for them, and joy
Will brim down.

15 With God

Who may dwell with you, Lord?
Or kneel in the sun of your love?

Only those who inhabit integrity,
Whose hearts harbour sincerity,
Who do not devise depravity,
But love all about them.

Only those who dissent
From double-dealing,
Who are attentive to truth,
Prize innocence, do not
Exploit need or poverty.

Only those who stand by their word,
Who do not lie with liars or
Turn the tread of justice. Only those
Who live towards God.

It is to these the Lord reaches out.
It is these he takes to himself.
Disinclined to loneliness, he – though
More than all – seeks all.

16 Joy in God

Lord, you are the joy of my soul,
The delight in my life.
A safe haven sheltering me.

The faithful, whose lives are
Consecrated to you, guide me.
Their fellowship inspires me.

I will turn from what is alien to holiness,
Invoke no powers that imperil,
No blasphemies which estrange.

You sustain me with plentiful harvests
And give fine grazing.
You have become my inheritance.

In the cool of dusk, the dark of night,
You are present. Secretly, in love, you
Come to bring me to lowliness.

Such communion draws my eyes to you.
Your beauty strengthens and
Makes me immovable in your cause.

You are mine forever. Your embrace
Brings my spirit from the ice of old deaths,
A grave of black flames.

We walk together along an unmown track
Younger than tomorrow; my life bursts with joy.
Your presence is unbounded rapture.

17 My Hope

Lord, you look truly.
See my innocence and honesty,
Confirm my cause, bring justice.

Should you surprise me among
Decaying nights, see, my heart
Is pure, my lips true, my way your way.

I seek you and you come to me.
You have become a beautiful harbour
For me and bring stillness to my life.

You keep me as one who inhabits your heart.
In love we lie together in a secret cave,
Hidden from marauding mobs,

Though, pitiless, they dog me still. Always on
My trail, they prowl about. Callous, they set
Snares, plot to ambush and drag me off.

Lord, waging war against me, they are servants
To passion. Obsessed with excess, they
Desire evil and its kin. Act for me against them.

For my part, I will live my life within
The loveliness of grace; beyond that
I shall awake tomorrow in your now.

18   King David's Thanksgiving

All my delight is your presence, Lord.

You come to me in love as the cornerstone of life,
As a pillar upholding me, the foundation of a citadel.
A saviour plucking me from traitors

Who besiege, who bring blindness to my eyes,
Ropes for my wrists, nightmares to my mind.
They haul me deeply. Deafening chaos. Hell!

In terror I scream out. From the throne of holiness,
You hear my torment. At their atrocities your fury
Floods over.

Earth shudders. Rocks convulse. Glaciers crack.
Foaming avalanches sever valleys. Craters flame.
You, the Lord, move.

From the far place of your dwelling,
In dense and raging storms, on fast-winged winds,
You, the Lord, come.

Unseen, billowing black, in ice-edged hail,
On squalls of searing ash, you speak
A voice of fire,

Which dredges to light an abyss of cliffs
Underpinning oceans, foundations shaped
In the tumult of earth's creation.

Enemies draw me down to howling waves.
But you plunge your arm to their midst,
Loose me from the surge.   . . .

You bring me to a secluded place and
Uncover my obedience, my trust. There you
Confer a true heart and bless my ways.

In love you come to your beloved.
You commend the faithful, the pure,
But detest those twisted with malice.

Your presence, a sun at night, gives courage.
Now I can leap trenches, scale walls,
Engage enemies eye to eye.

My beloved Lord is my soul's shield
And my vitality. He makes me
Swift to climb and strong to strike.

So I outrun enemies to the city, crush them
In the mire. They are dust from gutters,
Blown about by the wind.

He turns away from the backs of prisoners,
Deaf to evil. Yet victory is not mine – it is
A gift given by my Lord before

He anoints me to kingship over peoples
Unknown to me. Proud races submit, seek safety
With me, accept the Lord's authority.

Because he is invincible in battle,
Because his paths are holy,
Because, in love, he has taken me to his palace,

I will sing songs for him until music is played to silence.

19   The Way

I contemplate this. The Lord God stains with freshness
A cavalcade of spinning galaxies.
He tosses star blossoms across spiralling vaults.
Fingers stir a pool of gas – behold, Andromeda!

All that is, he creates. It reveals his artistry, thought.
Each opening day, closing night, discloses this.
It is glory further than words; majesty not said;
A vision to adore, in whose awe all people are still.

The Lord pitches a tent for the sun.
Like a shy bridegroom, he emerges from its canopy.
Like an eager athlete, he runs the circuit set
From morning's radiance to pale stars at dusk.

I contemplate the beauty of the Lord in his sun,
In the perfection of his way, stamped out for all.
It gives life and joy, refreshes the spirit,
Brings understanding to the simple.

Such a way, built on obedience, is a sun,
Dispersing gloom.
It is partner to justice, to truth.
Its only end is the Lord's caress of love.

Nothing compares to the way:
Neither the skills of creatures,
Nor their loveliness;
Neither human invention, nor wisdom.   ...

But in seeking you within your law,
I find frailty, deep within.
In mercy, from pride and wrongs
Forgetfully done, acquit me.

I wish to be blameless before you,
Pure in the language I shape,
The desires I cherish.
I yearn to delight you.

20 The Lord's Beloved

Because the Lord cherishes you,
He hears; so have courage, raise your head.
He comes, a secure haven
In which to shelter from those who harass you.

Because the Lord cherishes you,
He sustains you, his care for you is unbroken.
He remembers your loyalty, looks with favour
On the ways you choose to take.

Because the Lord cherishes you,
He will delight you with gifts to satisfy
The deepness of your living,
The longing of your spirit.

Because the Lord cherishes you,
Your friends will be overjoyed.
They will fly banners, shout your name.
Adore the God who hears your thought.

Because you are the Lord's beloved,
He slides aside what screens,
Assures you that in combat
You will conquer, for his shadow lies over you.

Because you are the Lord's beloved,
In neither troops nor weaponry, in neither discerning
Sages nor the power of sovereigns, will you trust.
Be steadfast, for your hope is in the loving kindness of God.

21   Chosen Ones

To you, Lord, not us, is the thanks given.

To you, Lord, not us, is thanks offered.
We celebrate your triumphs,
Rejoice in your saving gift.

For you crown those whom you elect,
Anointing them with life,
Satisfying their first longing for you.

You remain in their mingling years,
Enhancing reputations,
Blessing integrity, fidelity.

They stand – a steadfast
Homage – in your presence,
Their lives an augury of splendour.

But those who stand against you
Are consumed in the fire of majesty –
A princely power destroying shadows.

As field weed set for fire shrivels to ash
And, wind-blown, is ground in grime, so in
Death they have no franchise on the future.

Routed, archaic plots collapse; they dare not
Unwrap their thoughts before your splendour.
Now we can chant your high song of victory.

To you, Lord, not us, is the thanks given.

22 A Suffering Servant

Death menaces but you flee from me. I am alone.
Only red-tight hurt inhabits darkness. I am abandoned.
Prayers fall, unheard.
Gnawing nights stifle crying.
There is no answer – blank, flawed silence.

Yet each generation tells your love,
Trusts truth, finds hope in your shadow.
But I am slight, lowly, a butt for ridicule,
For the pitiless chorus of the mob.
Is this one in whom God delights? A son – stretched for vultures!

You watched over me from birth, laid me gently
To her breast. Do not push me aside, leave me to
Spiralling distress. Nightmares blind the horizon.
Blurred beasts race towards me.
All within me turns to terror.

Ghastly apparitions mass, pin my body,
Tear me naked. Impaling hands, feet, they back to
Mock agony. Anguish haunts. Pain overpowers
As life ebbs. Look. Remember.
Circle me in love.   . . .

Then I will shout *halleluias*,
Sing songs, give thanks. Wherever people
Gather, your name will be extolled.
For you are a God of the despised and distraught;
You heal hearts, quench thirst, give rest.

All who dwell on this globe are
Set within your compassion.
Nations and their peoples – wealthy and poor,
New-born and dying – come to adore.
You, saviour God, take them home.

23 Love

Not from a solitude of prison or incapacity,
But of high plains and wide skies,
My beloved comes to me.

Through a valley of unmown fields and cinnamon sun,
Where quails skirt their ways and white junipers grow,
My beloved walks with me.

Discarding a syntax of usage and convention,
In language bending beyond rule-bound borders,
My beloved speaks to me.

And unquenchable music, housed in the motion of stillness,
Distils to this: *I keep you in the lock of love's arms,*
For you are mine.

Though you are where phantoms scourge and doubt gnaws,
Where death censors life and torments truth, look to me
And I will stand with you.

My enemies, deflecting love and decorating barbarism,
Voyeurs of suffering and intimacy,
Surround me.

But they see that we celebrate and dare not intervene.
A meal of new bread and good wine is laid. The
Beloved kisses and crowns my head – for a

Space for love brings love. When knowing is breached
By eternity, when all days become one day, I shall find
The mystery of his uncalculating love.

24 The Lord Ascends

Zero is severed, time timed, stars dance.
Tectonic shifts vent oceans, lands heave.
A butterfly's ragged flight excites my baby.
These are the Lord's, his delight.
He encircles creation, though –
Cloistered in narrow grammar –
We cannot say it.

Who may come and worship him?
Those who are merciful, who beat down sin,
Who are pure in conduct and motive.
Those astonished at tangents of the holy
On the curve of flight and still-standing stone.
For God breathes his mystery
To wet their eyes.

Ancient doors, used to kings and festal rites,
Swing open for your matchless Lord.
Triumph and victory are emblazoned
On palms and feet.
He ascends for a coronation,
Taking his throne in the wing-beat
Of triple glory.

25 Remember Us

All that I am, could be,
Bends on your breath.
Come, shape me to love's ambition.

Desolation snares, tenders me to my
Enemies and their brittle allies.
Fear flays my spirit.

Give seekers – minstrels of incessant doubt –
Hope in the voice of life, a homecoming
In your unfamiliar presence.

Justice you immure in our hearts and
Lives, from the garden-time to now-time.
Knowledge of you, nailed to
Love – always unfinished – and
Mercy, directs halting indeterminate lives.

Now I walk the homeless way
Of truth and inexperienced
Peace with your people.
Quick to catch the patchwork of earth, we
Run, seeking you in love's dark.

Save us from the intoxicating
Treachery of our foes – evil eclipsing being.
Untouched by sin and all its surrogates, you
Vindicate those who do not expect you.

We wait in the hushed lament of each day – for,
Except in the irrational guarantee of
Your love, we are vexed
Zeros.

26 Coming to You

As lovers breathe breath in their
Beloved, so you are sensible of me.
You cherish the spinning hollow of my life,
Aware that faith inflames my way and
Lights me to you, ever new-born.

I have withdrawn from intimates
Of an archive of evil, who bury
Undeclared shadows in bestial trenches.
Slow poison is their voice. Though errant,
Do not herd me to death with them.

Searing yearning inches me to your
Hospice, where majesty wears mercy's crown.
It is a place of delight, the joy of its guests.
There, before your presence, I will sing a
Song of love enfolded by love.

27 With God

From a lonesome city
I come to you, reft.
You greet me tenderly.
Your love suffuses
Blindness with light,
Infirmity with power,
Dying with breath.
You guide me to the beginning.

Now you unhouse
Enemies garrisoned in
Violated lands.
Though – in a
Cold fury of unthinking –
They fracture peace,
Annex mercy and devour hope,
I need not fear their withered triumphs.

Within your sanctuary is bliss.
In its inner recess an
Unspoken hunger is met.
Fingertips touch: impromptu breath.
My eyes yield to yours.
Holy passion is finely tuned.
Its every accent is
Sweetness and proportion.   . . .

Apprentice to love, my song is this.
There is a child's beauty
In your ancient face – pattern mine on it.
I learn slowly the canon of your ways:
Ingrain them in me.
I see your shadow: match mine to it.
Your love is jubilant,
A hope against the intensity of nothing.

Beloved, I pursue you to high mountain places
Where my love seeks yours.
Though I am of no consequence, hear my song of
Fractured dreams and urgent hope.

Do not snatch me up, return me to the malice
Of feckless crowds.
At a whim they uncover the tackle of torture
And rush to practise impeccable evil.

Rescue me from the secret snares of their progeny;
Reward them with the death of dark oblivion.
No cartographer can survey their last journey –
There are no paths to midnight extinction.

Though you do not hear the words of my song,
See the love and intention of my heart.
It is you on whom I wager my life:
Light illuminating my freedom.

Infused with trust, my song invades your tent;
You – who give point and purpose to my stories,
Showing to whom you will, the beauty of your face.
I catch it in crying.

29 The Voice of Glory

The Lord is coming,
Sons from his celestial court sing, for
They know the inside of glory,
Which is a holy presence.
Acolytes of light chant and fling
A playful profusion of star
Blossom over negated deeps.

He calls – a distant thunder –
    terse lightning stabs fugitive dark.
He calls – thunder gathers –
    deer and oxen give birth before their time.
He calls – thunder rumbles –
    the wilderness convulses, its caves close-crushed.
He calls – claps of thunder –
    trees in ancient forests spiral to the ground.
He calls – thunder crashes –
    in high ranges mountains stumble in panic.
He calls – thunder rages –
    oceans are moulded by the fury of primeval water.

Within the temple he is enthroned: all adore.
The king of glory thunders love,
Baptises the outwardness of things.
His glory is within reach
But beyond taking;
Present, though forgetfully
Perceived.

30 Love's Shadow

Quietly, as the shadow of a silent lover,
You watched my life emblazoned for its end
By those skilled in paradigms of pain.
Their obscenities render organs impotent,
One by one – though their dungeons
Desire not truth, not lies,
But white screams of unmeaning.

Quietly, shadow of a forgotten lover,
You left my side, withdrew to
Summer trees, for pride was my premise.
Yet I did not sink to carrion pits beneath the hills,
For the shadow of your secret
Love returned and drew me
From death's white lips, from my ending.

That night was glazed hard with pain,
A sharp intrusion, compacting hope to dust.
But now love's timid shadow brings
Joys to stripe my days, swell my dreams.
So I sing a darling song,
For you raise those whom you love
To bliss.

31 You Keep Me

A singular voice sounds,
A counterpoint of expectancy and surprise.
My being quivers, crackles with praise –
For you come in answer.

Enemies hold me: a ring of besieging barbarity.
They allow none to escape without hurt.
That I am
Is their sharpest irritation.

They have uttered vicious anathemas
To me, meshed pain with despair.
My life provokes their bestiality.
I know there is hope – but not for me.

Within this vicious carnival, they deride honesty,
Pillory love, punish goodness.
How my heart longs for the ease that lies
With your presence.

Always your shadow is unexpected.
It comes in judgement to punish
Those who fester in self-flattery;
In love, to save those who seek you.

Do not forget my face, for all that I am
Is committed to your keeping.
Now you smile, my agony turns
To spring's colour, to rainbows of promise.

32 Sin Forgiven

Vacant chairs leaned by empty tables,
Shutters clattered to their locks,
Mist obliterated light – and
I fled from you.

Moorings in holiness snapped,
Official anarchy concealed me.
In contempt of virtue,
Falsehood was the index of my faith.

Yet my misery was deep until,
In silent tears, I set my life before you.
Then you came to me –
With fire and forgiveness.

I learned discipline and
Was weaned from sin.
For you brought love, which laughed
And quenched my yearning with joy.

Friends, hear what I say.
Though deceits and dividing lusts draw you,
Do not bicker with good, bed with evil,
Lest terrors – daily stalking nearer – seize you.

Adore the Lord. Celebrate his love.
He has not hidden mercy, forgotten forgiveness.
Congregate with his children,
Collude with goodness.

33 A New Song

Sing a new song.

Grinding rocks and scraping wings,
Hissing grasses, sparring winds,
Join their music to the rhythm of your song.

A song of joy, not curved to inflection
Or rites of grammar.
Outside words it springs from love.

Your first pulse was *Let there be.*
And from the fecund vastness of nothing –
Oceans, lands, lights, snails …

Your song of sounds – of creaking, fluting,
Bubbling – is untamed and new-ringing.
Its truth proposes our lives.

But variant cries transgress your song.
You watch as nations murmur, plot,
Unrestrained by justice – and music.   …

You hear their incantation
To brutal gods, prelude to timeless
Masques of extirpation.

Their liturgy is a solemnity of evil,
So you throw them aside
To dwell in the darkness they compose.

Vibrant joy infuses my life,
My heart bounds as it catches anew
The soliloquy of your ancient song.

It is music of
Intimate unfamiliarity:
The ever-new song of love.

34 Thanks Given

Adore God, from house to horizon;
Boast in his shining, it riddles through all things;
Celebrate his beauty, ancient and fresh-minted.

Do his will, for his shadow tilts to you. Then
Every eye reflects his dazzling dark, his
Fizzing light, and sees him come to guard,
Greet and feast the neglected and needy.

Holy food, life of his life, he gives to all. Tasting
Its power, they hunger no more – though the pitiless,
Justly, are set aside, for pride closes their eyes to him.

Know this, my friends: you are God's radical delight,
Loved children whom he coaxes to his ways.
Maintain your quest for the singularity of truth,
Never let your vanity compromise with evil.

Open are his ears and eyes for those who love;
Plead with him in hope and humility. But the
Quick cunning, stubborn finesse, sullied
Revels of the godless infect his purity.

Sing, for God looks and comes to you. Now,
Though your anguish is deeply rooted, it is rooted out.
Unbroken is your spirit through his love unbroken.

Vain imperatives of evil, feral and smoothing,
Will become impotent, will be abolished. Now,
Exiles can return, the banquet is set,
Your garments prepared. Love's
Zenith embraces you.

35 Deliver Me

I am forlorn, forsaken; no one is with me.
My prayer is this:

Stand at my side, Lord. Return fury for fury.
Enemies, rising from a dark plain,
Hound me to unsounded deeps.
Immune from light, they dwell in gloom.
My birth provokes their hate –
My transgression is this: I abide in being.

Stand at my side, Lord. Return violence for violence.
I nursed my foes in sickness,
Interceding for them with my friends.
But skilled in evil, with unheeding hearts,
They tortured my flesh and
Wreaked destruction about me.

Stand at my side, Lord. Return the tyranny of tyrants.
Hold them at bay, Lord.
They are liars. Mediating false meanings,
Hallowing dark values, they prowl about me.
As sharp gales snap summer's final flowers,
Send them to nothing.

Do not stand aside. Return to my side.
Remit to my foes the horrors prepared for me.
Censure their mendacity, jostling schemes,
Which violate truth and drain trust.
Rescue all who seek your love,
Who sing of peace and tingling hope.

I know you will not leave me
Forlorn and forsaken, without support.

Sin seeps along fault lines of
Misdefinition and delusion.
In silence its poison
Destroy a man's moral rage.

Its dark ooze is his darling guest.
Secretly he submits to slavery,
Folding back midnight thoughts
To barbarity and convenience.

No consequence intimidates,
No responsibility deters.
Left are the deceits with which
He deceives others and himself.

Unhesitating in evil –
Forgetful of justice
And nemesis –
Like all sinners, he argues, *God is elsewhere.*   ...

But you are not.
Though I wake or sleep, your love encloses me.
Though I flee or rest, your love embraces me.
Though I fly with the stars, dream from the abyss,
Your love seeks me, finds me, takes me
To eagle-high mountains.

There your shadow shelters, welcomes me.
There, in your light, day to my sight, I see a light
Which is the light of light, the point of truth,
The beauty of being, the spring of love.

Do not place me with those who
Bear no connection,
Whose urgency is ancient sin.
The time to come is set:
Draw me to its mystery.

37 A Collection of Wisdom Sayings

Arrogant evil, flourishing in the place of honour,
    quickly dies as dry bark in winter's fires.
Believe in God, let your eyes love him
    and his silent word will home in your heart.
Commit each hour of your life to him
    and your integrity will shine as a midday sun.
Don't brood when evil is victorious, trust in him,
    know that patience opens his gates.
Eventually evil will be conquered; then look up,
    see children playing under his white sun.

Faith will sustain you when wickedness triumphs;
    remember, to the meek is promised an inheritance.
God mocks the cunning schemes of the wicked
    and laughs at the sharpness of their snares.
Helpless, the poor are threatened; then God
    breaks the weapons of sin in sinners' hands.
I know that the need of the innocent
    is worth more than the gold of the guilty.
Just as the Lord loves the blameless, so in
    broken times he will care for his people.

Know this: wickedness is like spring greenery
    which soon shrivels to summer's dust.
Lend to the unreliable and lose the loan,
    but see the blessed give graciously to the needful.
May you walk the Lord's way; on his path
    a rounding love will protect and guide you.
Never in all my years have I seen the good
    abandoned by God, pleading for bread.
Offences are now forgiven; look up and see the place
    of awakening where you shall be with love.   ...

Peace will dwell with justice, evil men will be forgotten;
  the good will endure to receive their summer dreams.
Quiet and true, the virtuous are hosts to wisdom,
  the voice of holy reason reigns in their lives.
Responsive to his will and obedient to his call,
  the righteous know the kingdom of the heart.
Sinners seek the lives of the good, yet God
  will not let them perish in that fire without light.
Trust the Lord, walk his way and
  your joy will be hope for his love.

Unworthy men feast but briefly in their airy villas,
  the tree's shadow lengthens and they are seen no more.
Virtuous people and their families walk in the light,
  in the procession of those whom the Lord loves.
Wickedness and those who practise it
  will be forgotten, as if they had never lived.
Expect comfort and blessings from the Lord,
  even when there are trials and splinters on your way.
Your refuge is the Lord, know that
  he longs for you in your longing for him.
Zeal for God motivates the holy, they are not lost
  for they stay in the secret place of his love.

38 Forgive and Help Me

Once I danced on green, on a sunshine hill,
But now grey guilt beats me down.
Stilled from a destructive delirium,
I lie hunched for censure.
Pain preys on my body.
Its nakedness is clothed with sores.
Each night I sweat tight fear,
Each day is hung low with anguish.
Unshielded and vincible,
I sip cheap vinegar.

Once I laughed – jittery lambs,
Joyous colts – for you met my yearning.
Do so again, though I bring no
Profit to you. Foes and friends
Crush my body, bind my heart.
Light deserts my eyes,
Voices sound no more in my ears,
My tongue makes no tracks for speech.
A wounded riddle, I drag myself here
For your judgement.

Once I touched moonflowers in cooling mist,
Now I wait at this precipice
In red of burning pain.
What festers on my body eats my spirit.
My tenancy of life nears its close.
As I wait, my enemies – whom I cannot desert –
Dig a grave and smile at my despair.
Lord, my nipped penitence is real:
Do not shrink from me.
Call me to you again.

39 I Am Nothing

In the cold sobriety of a winter's sun,
Slowly I determine to control the
Patchwork of my being, so I tie
My tongue and interpolate silence.

But my passion is not suppressed.
Ancient terror and ferocious
Conviction sack my spirit
Until I speak.

Bring again to mind, Lord,
How certainly we race to be forgotten,
Like little waves – born from the grey of
Wordless seas – visiting outcast shores.

Yet always I wait for your presence –
Though I have travelled far from you –
For in your forgiveness
Lies the resurrection of hope.

Punish me no further.
Do not parade me – a
Paradox – before
The bitter scorn of my enemies.

I have no bright lodging
In this alien land,
So do not forsake me, Lord,
For I entrust myself to your keeping.

Impatient for love's light, I endured time's crawl.
Coming, you lifted me from darkness – nights of
Choking slime – and took me to sure ground.
You spoke to me, the voice of the sun chanting
A song of hope for day's grey dawn. I sang.

Lord, dismiss all who
Inflate fury to hide lies.
Draw close to me,
Ever eager for your shade.
A deep stillness
I am permeable to
The epiphanies of your love
In the fabric of each
Hour: sky-sand of
Broken stars, baby's breath.

Quickened to that
Not mine, I seek
To serve – but without
Numbing words or a
Profusion of promise.
I am here for your
Bidding, a witness to
The density incised in
Lives, to lesions of the spirit,
Which you mend.

Now spoors of sin criss-cross my life,
Twist me round. 'Loathsome,' people say,
Turning in disgust. Foes smirk. Return, forgive,
For in your gift of love, lovers are bound to you.
Come, Lord, I am impatient for love's bonds.

41 A Sick Person's Prayer

Stay with the stricken, stretch to the doomed;
For love to reach you, bless
The unblessed.

God's hand moves to guard guests, meet needs,
Heal your heart. He is beside you, holds you
In your deep sickness.

I wept a prayer to the Lord.

Enfold me before I am engulfed in the mire of
My sinning. Already enemies course about me
Shouting bitter taunts.

Cruel jesters stare, impatient for my death. My friends'
Comfort dries to an economy of the conventional, a banality
Of autistic gossip.

Even the friend my heart loved, a guest at my table, who took
Bread from my hand, wine from my bowl, comes no more. He
Has lost faith.

Now I am desolate, in raw pain. In love, which has no seasons,
See my love for you. Do not disguise tenderness as anger;
Reach towards me.

Book
Two

42 Thoughts of an Exile (1)

Love – an unchosen bond – summons,
And longing sears my heart.
Tracking you endlessly through this
Desert blaze, I ache for a voice of love.

On autumn's slopes
I watch the turtledove lament
His bride, born away
On the southern wind.

Dried out through many suns,
I linger for you, craving
Refreshment, the cool of
Your breath in my breath.

My anguish is love's question,
Cruelly shaped by
This pagan scorn:
Where is your God?

In my dark I remember your light;
Joyful times when, with festive thanks,
We thronged the temple for
Hallowed hours with you.   ...

Though the darkness is deep,
My desire is deeper. Should love wither,
Life snap and spirits spiral
To self-delusion, I will not let you go.

I sit in sadness far away.
From a distant land
I see the peaks of
Snow mountains and am sad.

Chaos plunges through
Their cataracts, overwhelms me.
I remember love, in early light, in darkness.
Speak my name, remember and restore me.

Though the darkness is deep,
My desire is deeper. Should love wither,
Life snap and spirits spiral
To self-delusion, I will not let you go.

43 Thoughts of an Exile (2)

My enemies disguise despair,
Giving secret audience to the inhuman.
Negotiating with the absurd for
Deportation, cleansing, political trial and

Killing grounds. Their insanities eclipse your
Sun and give a new warrant to the arbitrary.
Their inferences are vacant, allowing
Conclusions which brand living as relative.

There is a surfeit of hope:
It is for them not for me.
You have abandoned me
To a black enigma, to nothing.

Still I wait for you to claim me.
I seek, in your presence, a light to walk
The mountain way to your towers.
There, at your highest altar, I shall rejoice.

Though the darkness is deep,
My desire is deeper. Should love spiral
To self-delusion, I will not let you go.

44 Battles Lost

Then,
Our epics extolled your love for us.
Our ancestors sang of your delight in them,
Of your gifts to them.

Your mindfulness, muffled in our fathers' thought,
    conferred staunch wisdom.
Your strength, fused in our fathers' arms,
    pulsated with power.
Bone was broken, sinews snapped. A land was
    taken for us, given by you.

But now,
We are evicted from your love.
Incessant echoes of the past beguile the present –
And you have gone from us.

We awake each day to a dark horizon arching
    our own requiem;
You have incised Disgraced on our backs and expelled us
    from the future;
The seers of night have infiltrated with the deft
    rhetoric of barbarism.
The bitterness of these things is a lament for love.   . . .

Yet,
The offering of today's love and
Our hope for a lodging in hope,
Is crushed, fed to jackals.

Allow us again to be welcome intruders
    into your presence,
For the commerce of love. In anguished patience we
    wait for you.
Confirm the hypothesis of the spirit: that love endures,
    seeking the rapture of response.
The vision of these things is our song of faith.

45 Song for a Royal Wedding

Within the quick of creation, I wean words
To sing psalms of a king's splendour.

Beauty, the light of broken stars, rests on you.
Grace on your lips transmutes songs: what is
Shaped by your spirit echoes within us.

Your hands receive the moods, the rhythms of eternity;
You are raised in tenacious servitude to truth;
You are anointed for the intensity of holiness;
Your head is crowned with a simplicity of love;
You are enthroned in yellow, green, ever-freshness.

A caesura in the ascending song, there are shifts in scents,
Colour, aroma of balsam, threads of flutes: and your
Bride, a hidden queen, fire from roses, is led to you.
Maidens dance, a constellation of fragile grace; and
You – unknowing symbol of mightier royalty – are glad.

At the circle of dawn, in a white palace, courtiers,
Guests from new lands, assemble in halls of ivory.
They bring gifts to nourish intuition, sustain sensibility.
They predict heirs who will hear prophets, follow visions.

May this psalm commend your spirit to the future, to one yet to come.

From the seared air of a black and white landscape,
This final Lord takes us to his fastness of love.
In its forecourt we become passionate accomplices.

Now there will be no fear,
Though wild stars implode, heavens burn in disarray;
Though earth convulses in the fury of primeval seas;
Though mountains impact, avalanches seize clouds;
For he knows us.

Rejoice! The Lord is God, delight in his embrace.
Our hopes walk with him, he harvests our dreams.
In his solitude sleeps what is yet to be born.

Now there will be no fear.
In the night's vigil God prepares his sacrifice.
Dawn shows his work – love set in the heart of
A city, refreshed by water from his holy river.
I know this: it is he who remembers us.

Rejoice! The Lord is God, delight in his embrace.
Our hopes walk with him, he harvests our dreams.
In his solitude sleeps what is yet to be born.

Put away fear, for he who clothes suns bridles
Those who darken vision, despise compassion
Extinguish the light of their generations.
Know him in the stillness, the awe of your self.
Love him: for he loves you.

Rejoice! The Lord is God, delight in his embrace.
Our hopes walk with him, he harvests our dreams.
In his solitude sleeps what is yet to be born.

47 The Enthronement Hymn

Throng the temple and greet your God
In songs and shouts with dance and drum.
It is he who binds the boundless,
And sees all that seeks to be unseen.

The peoples glimpse love's rainbow
Set within his eyes and adore.
From a passion for us, out of great emptiness
He shaped the fullness of our ground with his lines.

He comes, an elusive light lighting all things,
A truth the confluence of lucidity and awe.
Now music, predator of silence, completes what
Words must leave unbegun and will not echo.

He ascends his hill to be enthroned: his consummation.
All who see are tested in the tension of the sublime.
Time's continuity is wrested out, quickened to eternity,
Shifting a calculus of the daily to indwelling glory.

Throng the temple and greet your God
In songs and shouts with dance and drum.
It is he to whom all things refer.
He ascends into now with a simplicity of love.

48 The City of God

Our praise, the least cipher in your untold text,
Proclaims a city;
Its site, an ancient hill of victory;
Its centre, a pulse of living love;
Its borders, a counterpoint of joy and light.

We, our ancestors and children of tomorrow,
Proclaim you king;
You speak – a melody beyond any singing,
From whose mystery and music comes a
Sound captivating walls and ramparts.

Leaders of nations, coming to conquer,
Gather for war against this city.
But its shade is an epiphany that astounds;
A revelation from which, seeing only dry sand
Tossed to the tumult of the winds, they flee.

In the inner solitude of your temple, we stand
And contemplate the love, the hope you weave
In the margins of life's days and dreams.
Nascent faith dimly sees your gifts,
Knows that all we own is owed to you.

Then, as we circuit the city – citadels, battlements –
In jubilant processions, duplicity is pared away
And the narration of your steadfast love,
Enduring the durance of eternity,
Becomes our song.

49 The Mystery of Life

Hear me as
I try to keep the insoluble,
Fix the vehemence of its paradox,
Frame thoughts to disclose its curse,
Capture its haunting within the measure
Of a simple

Psalm. Life's question, ancient riddle,
That I know myself – and am known
To others only within my mortality – is
Posed again.
The possible clings to the cliffs of the
Impossible, then falls into blackness:

Always. Life makes no shelters for permanence: not
For the drama of kingdoms subverted by princes;
For the tall houses of the rich;
For the ancient understanding incised by the wise,
For the merriment of children, for fools' comedy.
For lovers' passion.

No. In death everything goes.
Nothing evades an epilogue, for
Life is not purchased at market benches
Nor ransomed by the solemnities of a courthouse.
Indistinct as shadows, our fury flickers,
Then a fire stutters to stillness.

Yet my experience is this:
God has set the upsurge of love in me,
It flames through the continuities of life.
When I leave my psalms for others to chant,
To take up what I leave, in joy and shining
I pray to be with him, take his fare.

From a recess of time at the rim of space,
The Lord calls, word from purest nullity.
Galaxies, on their scaffolding of night, withdraw as
The Lord passes, beauty his sovereign form.

His word energises and all the earth assembles –
Wild asses from the steppe, eagles from cliffs of sheer.
The Lord comes close to those who bear the
Servitude of his love. His charge is taut with necessity.

Conduct and thought are torn apart when you sacrifice;
In your oblation, action and meaning do not match;
Penitence is the tongue's convention, not a heart's conviction;
Prayers are an arrogant bluff, a convenience for pretence.

I see the word beneath words, the inside of speech;
So let integrity inhabit praise and honesty sworn vows.
For, beyond the possibilities of thought, distant from language,
I am God! Truth is my light and love my closest shadow.

He turns, censuring the pack at his door. *I know your guile.*
You mock meanings to strangle understanding, to trivialise
precepts.
Devotion shelters your profanity, hallowing curses,
Consecrating lies, crowning insincerity.

You have abused my silence – which is love's time, not yours.
Furtive and unforgiving, addicted to the arbitrary,
You cruelly bait and assail even your friends.
Know this: there is a time for judgement.

51 A Sinner's Plea

In the tender love I incite in you,
In its sublime singularity,
Live mercy, healing and grace.

May they loose me from all that binds.
For, though I walk in bright and busy places,
I wander aimless in an empty night.

I am far from you and my heart is barren,
For deceit and sophistry mark my life
And deaden prayer.

Dissimulation scrutinises each day,
Silencing the implications of the past.
Its dark chords negate your word.

There is no communion in converse with you.
Daily, the antics of jargon and triviality
Blur the urgency of my need.

Hope is fractured, dreams shredded.
Faith is a childish digression,
An unrhyming dogma.

But come. Run to me with forgiveness,
Return me from exile, renew me with
The tormenting intensity of love.

For you stock my life with promise,
Setting its motion within borders of joy. Now
It exposes the inconceivable – your love for me.

52 A Wicked Man

Why do you ignore landmarks for truth?
Why do you disdain gentleness?
An aureate swagger of rings,
Strutting gems, a mannered
Flourish of brocade
And a troupe of fawning friends
Cannot cloak the vitrine of your evil.

You vend sad dreams, blistering perfection.
Though your power is pervasive –
You are a virtuoso in guile –
Your dissent does not
Remove the Lord. The severe
Impeachment of his love reaches
From seaways to skyways.

You are not immune from the coercion
Of death. He sees the exhaustive
Commentary on evil your life
Inscribes and condemns you.
As for me, the Lord will love me like
An early cherry, breaking blossom
In the first summer breeze.

53 Cynics

Smart cynics dismiss his shadow – an irrelevance.
In denial dwells evasion, escape from duty,
Hostility to virtue.

But God lives with his people – illimitable love.
He weeps. Not one seeks him, not one
Lives for goodness.

People no longer understand words – *holy, God.*
They sponsor evil and, without conscience,
Ply sad plausibility.

Yet, unknowing, they stand in light – his grace.
He thwarts their schemes and reaches out to
His beloved ones.

He draws those who seek him – a remnant.
In times to be, he will be again for them, and joy
Will brim down.

54 A Prayer

Return to me, Lord.
From the still air of high ranges
Come to the wasteland within me,
For I am harnessed to a dispensation
Of abstention and division.

Lie with me, Lord.
For intimacy with you brings healing
From the density of my life,
Where I am hostage to dogmas
Scandalous to pity and grace.

Draw me to you, Lord.
Rout those who harry me to extinction's edge.
Call me by name.
Take my earthly sonship and
Transform it to a heavenly.

55 Friendship Betrayed

As pain twists to torment in my darkened heart,
I cry to the solitude of the horizon
For your shadow over me.

In a whirlwind that seethes and stinks, I am
Overtaken by enemies, abandoned by friends.
Crushed in terror, hope is wrenched away.

There are no escape routes. I cannot break loose
To dwell in the Pleiades, sing with new stars
Or fly with herons to the wind marshes.

I wait in the city where untruth ripens to theory;
I watch anonymous duplicity in the markets;
I see men nourishing an addiction to immediacy.

My agony swells to an unbearable rack, for in
Soft evasion you, my deepest friend, whose
Head leant to me, have wrapped me in treachery.

Now I see holes in your eyes,
Ambiguity on your lips, a heart with no
Passion – numbers scour out imagination.

But the Lord himself, against whom you are nothing,
Will come with the end. He will defy your pomp,
Dismiss your inventions – technology of butchery.

My trust is in God, who instructed my birth;
Who, though immutable, suffers; who, though
Infinite, will come to dwell with me.

56 Trust in God

The fault lines crack,
Children fall silent, saplings moulder.
The strategic hate of enemies
Shadows me, even to the high hills.

With policies, born from the
Imperfection of their dreams,
They deflect the present and barter hope
For a future, deep with black.

Steeped in an eschatalogy of evil,
With mannered words,
They pass sentence on me:
Death.

Yet God hears the shrillness, the lies,
Sees the fickleness of will
And brings their rebellion to its end:
Death.

I will invoke one in whose love I live.
He is not guarded from the hurt in creation,
He remembers those without name
Who remain in the night.

He knows my name and counts my years.
He takes my shoulder, walks with me to
His great hall and gives bread
From his loaf, drink from his cup.

57 He Delivered Me

To you I run, to westwards valleys, seeking sanctuary.
I am in peril, fast running from those in pursuit,
Those whose devotion to barbarity,
Dislocates my mind.
There is night-time on their faces.

I rush the stony tracks to you, a safe refuge;
For you are my solace in grief,
My hope in defeat, my life in death.
Only you, Lord, bring truth to my ear
And love to my heart.

Your spirit spans spaces further than stars,
Yet with wet-laced webs you delight children.

Now my foes are seized in snares set for me,
Victims of their own sport,
They saw victory in blood.
Now I hear the psalm of the children of light,
For the Lord who saved me.

Its sound is rooted in a rose of fire,
A mythical word, a *fiat* from the first air.
Its hermetic syntax stills to adoration. And
The reed flute speaks of pain in beauty,
A dark in the light of love.

Your spirit spans spaces further than stars,
Yet with wet-laced webs you delight children.

There are many in high houses, whose self-
Estimation and hauteur concedes they are gods.
They hold court to cripple freedom,
Hide justice and systematise self-praise.

Accepting no criteria of constraint or
Necessity in their descent to power,
They are principals in an arcana of cruelty,
Ruling through inhumanity.

But the Lord, who is God, is truth not to be
Bought – though he will buy them.
He watches their end. Soon they are dust between
Boards, on a beetle's wing, under a waiting stone.

At this, those scarred by the severity
Of louche judgements, rejoice in the God
Who heals their hurts. He brings from their
Suffering and need, equity and love.

59 God Who Delivers

In the twilight I stare at deep chasms,
Waiting.
They are as close as the distance of dying.
Darkness seeps through my eyes.
In a circle of torment, foes creep forward.

All night I hear the rhetoric of evil,
Hysterical anathemas uttered against me.

Anguish stands to the land's limit,
Waiting.
It leaches to my grey heart.
Feel despair brush your hand, Lord.
Turn. As an orphaned child,

I sing afresh of your saving strength
Towards those in whom you take delight.

Hooded killers, lies disguised as truth, are
Waiting
To take me. These ciphers, shadows, flawlessly obscure,
Draw me for their bestiality. With a host of suns, Lord,
Come against them; scatter this frozen gloom.

All night I hear the rhetoric of evil,
Hysterical anathemas uttered against me.   ...

You are my beloved, because of love you are
Waiting.
From love, you have taken me in love,
To share with you the life of love.
So again

I sing afresh of your saving strength
Towards those in whom you take delight.

60 Disaster

You have turned aside from us –
Outraged at a flowering evil;
You have abandoned us –
Outraged at the inventory of sin;
It is as if we, your children,
Were strangers to you.

So you called the earth
To heave in judgement,
Waters to split, fire to spout;
Only you can soothe this rage.
Famine is your birthday gift,
Poisoned wine your blessing.

Call forgiveness to us from your haven,
Imparadise our hearts. Speak love to us.
In the north is my bride;
In the south my son;
In the east my daughter;
In the west my beloved.

Turn with your censure
And curse our enemies. Speak this judgement.
For the north crumbling cities, blowing dust;
For the south barren soil, dying roots;
For the east an exile, without return;
For the west a wilderness, without rain.

When you are absent, Lord, we are broken,
Without victory. Come and we are invincible.
Then words shed their rags and naked
Meaning sparkles for us – without speech
But known, not heard but understood.
We rejoice, for you whisper to us in love.

From a far exile without return,
My spirit turns, tries to remember.
Enemies have led me through rivers
And sour places, by crude citadels in
New cities.

Yet in days is set your living presence.
At each dawning I kneel;
The time of the sun is here.
Its melody sustains, despite
Their ministries of obliteration.

Your love is my home.
In its secret cave,
In an intimacy –
From beyond –
Your tenderness is revealed.

I know now that old promises
Are true, that my people and
The king are blessed, that
You dance among us, for in
Time's heart dwells your holiness.

I wait in silence for the Lord, my beloved,
And ponder an inner sunrise of stillness.
After the night of limb-locked struggle – he
Did not crush me – he will
Come to sit with me as a true friend
And give me a portion from his plate.

Now the sun beseeches a greater to bestow
The day. In new light I watch my friends –
Who are enemies – race towards me with
Animal ferocity. Their blessings curse,
Their greetings scourge, their gifts are
A darkness giving form to fear.

Those who watch, waiting for desert's dawn, see.
We are shifting winds dwelling in distraction,
Dodging the eternal, limiting love.
Now, holding the fullness of day's light,
I see you are beauty I shall not own,
But to whom I may offer myself.

63 My Lover

You are a song my soul waits to hear,
But you are far from me.
This wilderness is a dry wall
Which separates me from you.

You are a song my soul waits to sing.
My heartbeat will shape
The grammar of its words
With love's emendations.

You are a song my soul waits to chant.
It will sound over the night ocean;
Skirting shearwaters will add
Their gloss of love.

You are a song my soul waits to tell.
But enemies stir hope to silence,
Set you outside determined
Bounds of the daily.

You are a song my soul waits to pray.
Piercing language, it is a worship
Enfolding little meanings in greater,
Catching beauty in the energy of light.

You are a song my soul waits to feel.
Its shock sets my joy free for an
Urgency – an unimaginable simplicity:
Your coming in intimacy.

You are a song my soul waits to hear.
I empty space for the space of love;
Then I am known in the unknown
And loved by love.

My mute lament is gripped
In a soft web's stretch, spun by
Those who hate me.

All that is left is horror
At an absence of horror
In their hearts.

Their alliance with evil hides
Your word in blank piety,
In arcane ceremonial.

Architects of cunning,
Their sinister lubricities
Blaspheme your laws.

A taut skein of ugliness
Draws their thinking, as
They plot my insanity.

But you see and reward
Their guilt. Now their path
Is to a lasting extinction.

But I rejoice. For at the close
Of words there filters a light
Which speaks of you.

Now light – the form of mercy,
Substance of love – inhabits my
Routine doing.

65 All That Is

The breath of sleepers sleeping, silence before song,
Spaces in our speaking, give praise to you, Lord.
All that is, is through you, from you, without forgetting.
We are fashioned by you, for you, to take berries, juice.

But there are few continuities, always new patterns;
We are far from ourselves, private, deep in defence.
Yet all that is, is through you, from you. But quickly
We turn away, to forgetting, to fussing in soft fear.

A metaphysic of rapture cannot measure your love
For us. It reconstitutes us for a holy ground,
Marked by you. Yet the mumbling of flesh, our high
Abstractions of fancy, parry your dreams for us.

You answer reserve – timid glances – with prodigality.
Sorrel, foxes, wrens and skate, Sirius and constellations,
Pathways to night are by you, from you, for you. Yet
We forget how to receive your stunning blows of beauty.

You conduct the stars, bouquets of shaking light,
Disturbed moons and crushed rainbows homeward,
For they are all by you, from you, for you. Crowned in
Early green, you shake it out over earth and seas.

The symmetries of space and sky, sonorities of deeps,
Each season's beauty – full fields of wild orchids –
Propose you. They are by you, from you, for you.
They whisper of ecstasies on the cusp of light.

The unfurling cloud, land swaddled in mist,
Sprouting rye on busy pasture, my child,
Are all by you, from you, for you. Everything
Sings of you: says love.

Then, before time, you slaked emptiness,
Unravelled nothing, filled the famished vacuum
And – by an irretrievable word –
Gave substance: wet and daisies,
Wolves and babies, deer and moles.

You stirred the cauldron of the stars, dark space
Was roused. From the whirlpool's edge swirling
Black and light entwined for you. Then you cut
The sea's place, sized the sky
And stretched a rainbow.

Your finger runs through time, guiding days,
Driving nights, necessity your pulsing will.
Mutinous history is our abstention from love,
Yet you stay to illumine thoughts,
To donate dreams.

Myrtlewood is laid on stone, rules remembered.
A sacrifice is sought – privation and oblation –
To scratch at your glory. Fire lives, kindled from
Slivers of holiness, but inadequacy remains our
Truth, our existence. Though

To action we grant vision, our hearts confer
Feelings at the shape of sacred sounds. May this
Sacrifice transfigure; nurture a greater love
Than I have known. Then, may I be
What I daily act.

67 Harvest Song

Grain trembling in summer storms,
Hair-grass bending in the rain,
Opportunistic poppies, bird-foot trefoil:
All speak of joy, a holy presence,
For you renew the world.

You come to all nations, to nourish them with hope
And refresh with mercy, to laugh with their children
And give seeds for sowing.

The word of love is born within your peoples,
A simplicity, generating and sustaining – here
And in every constellation.
You set fields; warm the grain and grapes;
Offer bread to nourish, wine to quench.

You come to all nations, to nourish them with hope
And refresh with mercy, to laugh with their children
And give seeds for sowing.

There's beauty in chance findings, gauzy
Lacewings, a waiting stone, whitening bones.
There's grace brimming in provision
Of thyme and straw, beans and honey. As there
Is earthly meat, may there be heavenly bread.

You come to all nations, to nourish them with hope
And refresh with mercy, to laugh with their children
And give seeds for sowing.

68 A Song of Triumph

In ancient power, God comes to his temple.
He scatters rivals indifferent to holiness.
His friends dance as new promise dawns.

He rides in deserts – bright on white.
Remembering unrecorded, vanquished lives,
He calls out to those for whom there is no return.

Locked in the savagery of shifting depths,
Rocks gush as he passes by. He gives those
Whose earthly cause is set aside, everlasting hope.

Anonymous kings stalk him to death-traps.
But he lays soft snow, white on white, and
Routs them, for evil shadows their tracks.

His procession of yoked princes stretches to
A midnight horizon. No longer will they plot to
Take him, trade honesty for success, tradition for fact.

He gives battle spoils – pigeons of pure gold,
Silver circlets – to infants, to those in peace. These see
Him, embedding eternity in rapids of the present.

Sky's fanfare shouts: a crescendo of song from those in
Whom he delights; a chant whose ancient text is refreshed
By children's laughter. He summons his loved ones.   . . .

His procession enters the sanctuary. He hears a
Recitation of his loving kindness; his conquest of all
Who seek the naissance of inhumanity, black on black.

The end, a liturgy in silence: awe before majesty,
Astonishment at beauty, humility before mystery;
A liturgy of silence, speaking love to the beloved.

69 In Deep Sadness

Braced to time's wall, pain is my focus,
Death's dark crawls closer each hour.
There is no sun: but despair.
I call: you are absent.

Sin incises my life,
Claws through thought.
Do not forget me, rinse me
Away like night's dreams.

Love for you exposes me
To the loathing of enemies.
I am powerless against their abuse,
The disorder they imagine.

As the grey pelican cries for her love
In a profitless desert, I call for you.
Answer me: I choose no other than you.
Your beauty is my delight.

Foes mock my call. They practise
Evil – from a lexicon of depravity –
Against me. It is unspeakable.
I seek comfort: but know agony.

Senses scream. Talk cannot inflect
This horror. They propagate fires
On me. Expel barbarity and havoc
With your judgement.

And now I wait for you.
There is nothing else.
Just an expectation of love,
Given to me by your love.

70 Be With Me

There is no one to hold me,
No context for my life.
Conventions collapse,
Markers are rubbed away
And lights snuffed.

Prayers, from your words,
Do not reach.
You are to high for me and –
With unimpaired integrity –
Persistently opaque.

Enemies write my name
In the register of death.
A magma of sinister logic
Overwhelms. Trip them
By their own schemes.

As a father closes the eyelids
Of his child with a kiss,
May you lean to your people
With the fire of your love: yet still
There is none to hold me.

71 The Old Sing

You give speech when speech fails;
You bring strength when hearts ebb;
You change the ash of death
To a fire of life and take your
Beloved to cloud-high dwellings.

Come again, for it was you who brought me,
Without coincidence, undisturbed by time,
To birth. My early love, raw love,
Was fashioned for you. Hear me still in
Late love, when dreams collapse.

The faces of my enemies bring
Smiling lies and long agony.
Too quickly I am too old and
Without acquittal. They baste my body
And check my breath for death.

But you care for crumpled hair
Wisped in white and sweat.
Into my dwindling days,
Insensible to seasons and distinctions,
Oozes your glory.   ...

Though autumn is at my back and
Winter comes, my tongue is
Stamped with the word of love.
And love's necessity unwills
Servitude and futility.

No one unravels the exegesis
Of the holy, no tropes tell your splendour,
There are no masks beneath the skin.
So I stand in stillness and my heart
Sings a silent song.

72 Praise the King

The urgent bright of the sun's light
Rounds about your son, Lord, and reflects
Blue gentians in his eyes. His are
Young hands, scarred, redressing wrongs;
Young feet, wounded, walking to peace.

Your prince, a midday blaze and orient presence,
Looks out: eyes meet on the errands of love.
He blesses the congestion of life
With justice, with joy. His energy holds the world:
Frosted sedge, drips of lazy rain.

His vision reaches to a nothing before beginnings.
To those he meets he brings his gifts:
Of goodness brooding in their bones,
Of questions building the future,
Of melodies haunting far thoughts.

To kings, he offers a freedom to serve;
To the poor, humility to achieve an impossible;
To priests, a knack for knowing
The cracks in logic's sour face;
To children, fingers to find bindweed, honeysuckle.   . . .

Now as in ancient times, summer's in the spring,
Mountain's in the valley and day's in the dark.
Creative grace brims over: crazy butterflies,
Serious ants, green figs uncertain in the
New sun, and old dogs sniffing.

Your submissive king sets love in the present.
In him all things – ladybirds, bread – make reference
To what is other, greater than themselves, sublime.
He brings failure to fullness, futility to redemption,
Making of death a homecoming for his people.

Book Three

73 Only You

I know that yours are the hands of flame
Tearing down and building.
But doubt reaches out in stealth and
Wraps me round, a dark mist before the day.
Its damp clothes me in envy, in fury.
For I dig among stones, chew thorns,
Yet in summer retreats evil men feast
On the fatness of lamb and sweet grapes.
Their thought is rancorous –
The vaunt of wealth scoffs at piety.
They do not hear sounds within,
The moon is blank and soil unseen.
They say you are uncertain, inattentive,
And – like summer hail and children's
Dreams – metamorphose to inconsequence.
I lapse to fragile agreement,
A consent born from sickness and ill.
But pondering before you,
I watch the nemesis of infidelity and
Awake, my ignorance mended,
For they are structured to destruction.
Words, wind-winnowed, fall away.
The fluency of stillness tells of you:
Silence is the proposition of truth,
A proof in the theorem of love.
So in quiet I cup a shell to my ear.
In the chant of the sea's surge
Is the surprise of love's memory
Eternally dancing with me. Now
Love for you lacerates my life,
Is my perilous companion,
Is everything, all that I can seek.

74 Save Us

My heart is numb, the sky still, seas silent.
We are pushed to one side, rind at a plate's edge.
Time is rent and love torn, for we are unwanted.

Enemies have overturned memory, imagination;
The future has fled, we have ended.
Hating you, they have harnessed their gods for war.

Your dread sanctuary is transfigured to night,
Its beauty effaced in a monotony of dust,
Liturgy tuned to scandals of barbarity.

Kin are with corpses. We are naked, washed
For the grave. Wisdom transmutes to irony,
Prophecy is censored. Must this time remain?

You took the bounds of nothing, bursting with an
Unconceived; set banks of black at the rim of space;
Cast lights of the night; led the day to her rest.

You called ibis, antelope, wild ass. They appeared.
You walked the sea's groves and loosed whales;
You gave meaning to thought, sound to words.

Yet enemies imagine an unimaginable – death.
They have not met mercy or seen pity.
Those absent will not believe these things.

Will your patient love sift ash and remember us?
Will you restore your sanctuary and our hearts?
Will you give an answer to cure our sadness?

75 Our Judge

Earth and heaven hold nothing
To match your name, Lord.
Symmetry and rhythm,
Beauty and proportion
Spill over,
Yet glory is yours.

You say to evil men,
I will give sentence against you
Because you have rebelled,
Harboured nightmares
And become versatile
In the archive of evil.

Wherever they look for help
The horizon is stern, empty.
Though they are deft in barbarism
And shameful governance,
Dividing truth,
The Lord God is not subverted.

As in the first times, he marks our road
And brings justice, a chalice of red,
Frothing to the brim.
Foes drink for death,
But we are drawn to intimacy for
His mercy comes early upon us.

Whatever, be the lighter brighter
Or the darker denser;
Whatever, if I am sick to die
Or live to joy, no matter;
For when I am far off
You will see and run to me.

76 To God

Among us is the presence of God,
A severe and stretching love.
Among us is the beauty of God,
Motive and goal of longing.
Among us is the stretch of glory,
Spanning unsounded space.

Those who menaced you,
Filled with vengeance,
Were powerless in the place of battle.
Nor did they know that
When the small die, there is no pomp
And the harvest does not stop.

None may intrude upon you, Lord,
Transgress the edge of definition,
Bear your vision, surpass you in
Enduring dark as black gathers blackness.
I remember that the poor, the sick, the children,
You wrap in hope, in cloud-blossom.

It is you we contemplate,
As the river of light seeks its nativity.
It is you we desire,
For the love of being is the proof of Being.
It is you we seek;
Only you can draw the sting from our hearts.

77　A Suppliant's Unfinished Prayer

In desert grey before day's light,
Before the heron feeds her chicks
And toads awake, I gasp for you –
Grief has taken my voice.

I kneel on unfriendly sand, lift my arms.
I search tracks among the rocks, reed beds,
In hostile gorges, but they are silent of you.
Their stillness chokes. My heart is checked.

Has the Lord unfolded his coat: left us?
Is his face cold, hard like ice-braced fields?
Will he return before my eyes close to sight,
My heart to remembrance?

Sorrow exhausted and patience dead,
I lie by trim graves, pondering your glory –
In time and season, sustained for
A thousand years: present in this hour.

Give me the voice and speech to sing it?
No. For he – wary of white-distempered
Prayer – has adjourned the task of words
For the practice of silence.

Though I am abandoned, maimed by the palsy
Of age, I will still stammer praise to life's edge.
Before you, idols – inert proxies for feelings –
Tumble and perish. With you love is born.

Love was in your heart first, when space was
Uncoiled, stars spun in rumpled galaxies;
When you walked beneath seas, through
Deserts, to set your children free to be.

All my minstrelsy sings one song. An unfinished
Melody, it awaits those to come.
Begun by ancient graves, it speaks of loss,
The lineaments of love, hope kindled in a wilful people.

It tells of the Lord God, his kindly dower, self-gift
And stubborn promise, of the consent of love once given
By that people to his kingly rule – created to creator,
Child to parent, beloved to lover.

Expectant, he worked his wonders, longing for their longing;
Faithful, he drew them dry through a fickle sea, shaping trust;
Tenderly, he led them in waste places to see sublimity.
Silently, he taught them to hear the word in stillness.

Through the long night – dark night – of their generations,
He kept a vigil over them, wedding his will to theirs.
He waited for them to tear apart the past,
Become a place for his indwelling.

But they faltered, attuned themselves to themselves.
Unable to sing the new song hidden within or dance
His measure, they did not notice his face.
Displaced, they sought exile without hope. They had

Hissed Yes to old patterns, imagined a new idol: death.
Tides ebbed, winters' cold rolled out night, defeated light.
In cunning secrecy, shadows – familiar with the grammar
Of lies and ingenious in equivocation – coiled about them.   ...

So the Lord God held us, naked, before his truth;
He chose us from the poorest and smallest: a remnant.
He smiled on us, blessed our need, gave help for hope;
He cherished us, chosen for an annunciation of love.

He came to us; gave a banquet of honeycomb and wine.
We received to give; saw the delicacy of love and purity.
Turtledoves sang at midnight, a fig tree blossomed.
The time of rejoicing returned. From death: hope.

79 The Destruction of Jerusalem

We are swaddled in nightmares and flames;
Violence is etched into days and life.
What is seen may not be said – yet not to say
Poisons words, fractures the world. So speak.

The place of your presence is defined
By dry ash, slashed lemon-wood,
Crushed bone, shattered slate
And the withered eyes of children.

Enemies cargo a final dereliction,
A black without height or measure,
Stark, unabating a bitter fury and
A massive negation mocking you.

In its hideous chill lies the implosion
Of hope. In a panic of undoing, we hear
The pitiless antinomies of death saying,
You, Lord, are remote. And we are alone.

Avenge the unmaking of your making!
I know the fervour of your love let loose
Topples foes and mends fragments,
Makes things sound and mint again.

80 Restore Us, Lord

Love led his beloved,
His children, with gentle reins
To new dwellings – for ruin?

Let the corona blush.
Come: a final singularity.
Come: the lightness of love.

Wrenched from our ease
We ate poisoned bread,
Quenched the present with blood.

Let the corona blush.
Come: a final singularity.
Come: the lightness of love.

From a gaunt, grey exile,
You drew us with your brightness
To prosper in daisy suns.

But the arc of winter enemies
Brought us to the edge of brokenness,
To seamless contradictions, to pain.

Mend what moths and greed eat,
Renew what expedience and power corrode,
Recall your dreams for us.

Let the corona blush.
Come: a final singularity.
Come: the lightness of love.

81 A Festival Hymn

For our God, unravel rejoicing!
Sing songs of joy!
Saturate his festival with a music
Born before stars, outlasting memory,
A sound that strips off old speech
And resonates past reason.

Now, in new syllables,
He ruptures knowing, says,
I took you from what you were not
To bring you to what you are.
Across uncertainty I led you
To an abiding identity.

Water and thunder, bread and pain
Were your given companions.
But you did not remember
Mothering arms enfranchising
Your lives and hopes, decoding days,
Dreams and the tangle of sense.

Your steps ached down smooth avenues
To idols: easily pleased and polished.
Return! Awaken half-forged memories
And know me – in echoes of unfamiliar
Love, in the grace of day's drift;
Both seeking to nuzzle you into eternity.

O Lord, come in purity to be our judge.

And the dreamer saw the dead –
Who colonise the edge of night,
Denied lodging in tomorrow's hope –
Plead against oppressors.

The Lord heard and appointed
Judges to press his law.
He saw a cleft in their piety:
They silenced love's demands.

His holy imposition required
Love's concretion.
But they licensed lies and the
Grim redress of vengeance.

They shed mercy, pillaged truth,
Exchanged justice for power.
Indifferent to tragedy, their courts
Were showcases for subtle evil.

The Lord saw abstract deceits
Branding their eyes – sight gave
No insight – so he cancelled their
Lives and brought them to death.

O Lord, come in purity to be our judge.

83 Enemies Surround Us

Lord, hear the crabbed lament
Of our abandonment, our dying.
This dimming light veils a
Horror hemming us round.

Your enemies speak with
Furtive duplicity. They smile:
And silently seek our ruin
In a turmoil of lies.

From uplands and stony plains,
From deserts and dark valleys,
From sea and land, they come
To bind holiness with flames.

Silence the drab murmur of their
Evil ways, the clannish sound of
Their timeless plots, for they break
Our freedom to follow you.

Let the winds waste their words,
The sun dry their passions
And your justice drain their lives;
For they have no home in you.

84 A Pilgrim Hymn

Like homing bees, sunset-spangled,
We are returning. Without you, kisses are lost,
Eyes unrewarded and there is no heart's ease.

With you, we will laugh at corncrakes,
Sing with the wishes of our children and
Delight that what has been can be again.

Translucent sacraments: conch and cowrie,
Calligraphy of leaves and wings, are
Flecked with glory and feed us with joy.

Through deeps and darks we travel to you.
Our road rejoices with us. Now its uplands
Unfold to the spindrift and greens of paradise.

Know my ardent longing for your breath.
Shade the secret recess of my spirit with your
Shy presence – pivot of life, measure of love.

The past is present with us; your love is our future.
Always remember us: we remember you always,
Pivot of beauty, whirlwind of giving, death of dying.

In your pavilion, sharing stories of hurt, of
Grace, we wait before you; we adore, sensible
That we are overtaken, overthrown by love.

85 A Prayer for Peace

In the green time of history,
Before the sun was broken,
Our children laughed,
The land was impatient
To give grapes and herbage.

You smiled on us,
Original among peoples;
Smeared the sky with rainbows;
Forgot your anger and
Hid wrath in a far place.

Smile again, pierce faith's obscurity;
Cherish us, repair our madness;
Strip us for freedom.
Come: wed peace to justice,
Mesh goodness with love.

God hears this supplication and speaks.
I will make you blazons of light,
Conscripts of glory. You shall hear
Afresh words that bring salvation,
Know the creative pulse of judgement.

No longer will you trespass between
Promise and fulfilment, for I will walk
With you. The invisibility of eternal
Love will come to kiss each new-born
Child and embrace your generations.

86 A Lamentation

Daily, faith is purged from me
And life ceded to guilt.
My account is never settled.
Exiled and hostage, I sing;
To you I bend my spirit;
In you I place my hope.

Had I seeing further than sight,
Hearing greater than sound,
Knowing more than wisdom,
I could not tell your story.
Nameless, it bypasses thought and
Doing in the spin of holy stillness.

So I will not speak – for
Vanity seeps through words.
What life cannot discern
My soul will embrace, for
I am made to love, and you
Give love its possibility.

Suave enemies raise a platform
Beneath my body – traduced
Carrion for kites and foxes.
Deliver me, for my life is a
Tattered banner which only
Love, only you, can grasp.

87 A New City

Your city rises: meaning
Emerging from the
Scepticism of time. It is an
Apostle of visions and dreams.

Love stays there: a primary
Coming, an invariant presence,
The welcoming hope
Of renascent life.

In it you cradle princes for far isles,
Fair wooded lands, great seas and
High ranges; anoint them for the task,
Extravagance and pain of love.

You house the unhoused,
Beget inventors, create
Knowledge and rupture death with
The exuberance of renewed life.

Singers, dancers – tenants of
Freedom – are the city's summoners,
Exegetes of this holy text:
Sacrifice is your heart's love.

It is my night.
Reliable phantoms scourge,
Doubt burns, memory torments.
Death censors life. Deflects hope.
Draws voyeurs to the stake of
Red pain you set for me.

No comfort. No gloss
Of ease deadens the clasp of
Torment. Briar-thick shadows – fixed
First to the boy – remain,
Hardy intruders signalling
Your absence, your derision.

Fused to misery, my life breaks:
You are inaccessible to me.
I am unanswered, abandoned,
Enmired in dread. Unheard,
I fall to the uttermost depth
Where suffering is conceived.

I am alone.
Breathing thins to anguish,
My skin has no reprieve
From ripening plagues.
Forsaken by my own,
I lie here in the grey of crazed days.

89 A Crisis

I sang of a love – penetrating privacy for
The exchange of life – I dared not predict.
It escaped lineation and sense and was
With this people, an elect people, and their future.

I sang of you, who set their vigil – and
Summer's yarrow, cloud-banked and cream,
And unfurled stars, opal and ochre – to
Outwait patience and bide for bidding.

I sang of their story – a chant of cost and loss,
Dispossession and death transfiguring
Understanding to faith –
Implicit with the light of justice.

I sang of their fierce beauty – golden words
To crown kings, their children's future,
And turn a memory to hope again – bare
Black trees against a purple-blood sky.

But now I lament those padlocked
To deep destruction, beleaguered
By exile, who choke on silence, who –
Placed on love's side – find it a cruel art.

My lament is this: the brilliant nightmare
Is real, scars multiply. An unspeakable is
Whispered, an unthinkable performed. You
Forgot us, Lord. Love fled. We die: again and again.

Book
Four

We are peoples who indwell the burning light of your eyes,
With whom you have lain in an intimacy of love through
The generations.

It is you – who cast time in the cup of your hand and
Marshall an unmasking of bare-limbed mountains – whom
We worship.

Our hearts throb, we grow old completely – without appeal –
Till silence ushers in a malignant, hugging halt, and owls and
Clouds die.

But as you, the ancient ever new and newly beautiful, stoop
To finger frosted dew, millennia pass and our dreams swiftly
Slip away.

The coin we have – an infinite particularity without return –
    is
Quickly spent, though not deciphered, before sin sends us to
    a
Sour close.

It is a strange grace to catch the implications of limitation –
A plaintive chant from the underside of leaves and the rank
Of nettles.

Our brief days – gifted for life – pivot monotonously round
Taboos and masks, deflecting fact and sensibility, dismissing
Your anger.

But let wrath stay with yesterday. Run to forgive. Give sight
To see a daystar dawning on us, sign of love's promise, hope
    of
New birth.

91 God's Protection

Unbidden, a summons brings me
To a strange, dissentient place where
The light of love's unreason lies.
It is a place, a secret place,
Set by the Lord who feathered space,
Where his shadow breathes.

It is a place of white light at midnight
For there the sun does not tire or die.
There I learn his rhythm: seeding,
Loosing, creating, breaking.
He unveils my ancient yearning,
Attunes my little breath to his.

Encircled by love's law, I do not
Fear the fact of hours and days.
No shards of dread or deep despair,
No pains of power or lame renown,
No easy arcs of human praise, stretching loss,
Can raze brave dreams or gyve time's hope.

His summons is specific.
Though an anonymity of dust, I am
Chosen for a love that knows no recess.
In fullest measure it soaks the universe.
Unacknowledged, it shapes me:
While I strain to possess it.

He is my safeguard from grotesqueries
Of war, of tactical deaths on sandy flatlands,
From conscripted love and leaking thought
Clawing me to the bounty of a grave.
He is God, his touch is my life, his gift is grace
And the silent beauty of salvation is his word.

Snare imagination to mine my song –
A play of possibility awaiting life –
For day and night the song I shape is yours.

Let your beauty balance antimonies
Of form and substance in its
Motion, its rhythmic incitement,

Making music – a barrier of light –
Porous to the insinuation of
Your ancient and agile glory.

I sing of energising shocks in creation;
Of mysteries prior to the surge of words:
Rain, dogbane, child, oblation, death, love.

You remain the untameable mercy –
Between, beneath, the words of song –
Bringing green to the run of my years.

When night comes, the keeper
Of the vineyard locks the gates.
Without, the wicked wait forever.

But for me you lift the latch and
A smothered silence of yearning
Is transfixed in love's chalice.

93　The Grandeur of God

Day's down, sky's lid lifts,
Eyes deepen in the dark majesty of space.
You bunch stars for extinction,
Roll galaxies to silence,
From nothing provoke a contradiction:
What was not, is.

From a potency of absence
You enact a presence of ling,
Green-cream clover, crested grebes,
Swirling waters, gnawing cliffs,
Crying lips, loving lives:
All in an inessential prodigality.

You are the one words dare not report.
Trapped in neither language nor thought,
You appear in a swirl of egrets' wings.
You are prior to distinction, separation,
Yet spiders' eyes know your circuit, and
Each human life seeks your way.

Like late autumn bees heavy for death,
We falter to the earth.
Enemies – practising an archaic, dark-
Veined evil – take us,
Lead us to a place of liquid night,
Dense, black, bitter.
We choke and end.

Trapped in hate, a bound freight
Sightless and accursed, dragged
Through nights to night,
We are a mirror's image of the end.
There is no sanction, no rescue.
The Lord does not speak.
He has gone, they say.

Impotent rhetoric!
Fools destroying words.
How will he, heard in each sound,
Be silent?
How is an eternally present absent?
How will he whose being
Is love, cease loving?

Though they blank out crying,
Lord, come from shadows, sear
Their barricades of cruelty,
Disturb raw feasting. Then may
Your love – obdurate enigma –
Restore innocence,
Transfigure tragedy.

95 Rejoice!

Rejoicing, we seek to sing
A song more than itself,
Lacing a heavenly word to an earthly.
Two words, single yet
Fusing to an unfledged form,
To a time and a psalmody
Unsegmented for beauty.

Lord, you breach nothing
To extract what is:
Earth's hills bowing to dust,
Crack and split of apple-wood fires,
Trackless ways under ocean's night,
The lock of lovers'
Leaving.

We adore you: breath imaging us,
Creation overspilling moulds.
You speak. *Stand aside*
From the pitch of pride.
Know the dues of sin.
Wait in penance.
Turn homeward.

Swell my words with light;
Heighten, magnify,
Re-shape my songs –
But in a holy register.
They ponder his name,
They bless him for who he is:

A strength to cull the heavens,
A deftness mending time's ache;
A pulse to drive the breaking moon,
A breath for bustling leaves.
A beauty seen in plovers' eggs,
A motion in the arc of days.

He conscripts nations to justice,
Gives redress;
He measures equity among them,
Licenses good;
He unravels their freedom,
Aligns them to love.

In haunted spaces the Lord comes.
Earth – stamped with joy –
Rejoices, and seas and trees sing.
Tingling we live before him,
In adoration we empty ourselves –
To become ourselves entirely.

97 Love and Beauty

From this temple to furthest isles,
Uncharted coasts, unseen seas,
You are Lord.
From this temple to new suns
Veiled in the slow measure of space,
You are Lord.

The earth's round of colour –
Nodding hare-bells and white,
A flight and flash of kingfisher's light,
Green-grey oceans' sighing surf –
Reflects the beauty in your eyes.
Behold us in the eye of beauty.

It is your herald,
Evangelist of glory,
Life's golden purpose.
Revealed to peoples in the rush
Of history, it is image and
Substance of a creator's love.

In love's surrender, light and joy
Are born, children seeking life with us.
Thanksgiving is silent for –
Impenetrable to inquiry,
Inimical to mimesis –
You are Lord, the very beauty of love.

98 My Song for You

My song stops at a stale frontier.
Words repeat, breathe no sequel.
My round of sound seeks fresh tones,
A fledgling stress, harmonies from
The density of glory, to sing for you

A song budding to celebrate a victor
Whose arm halts time's narrative of pain;
Burns the subtle grammar of hurt;
Raises justice to peace; and
Stays slow deaths.

Every song I sing, sings of you
Whose finger turns the tide's recess,
Stirs dog whelks, roots sea campion by the shore.
Your breath shapes chants whose symmetry
And simplicity no flutes play or scripts record.

Your only song is love, ever love.
It sings the unborn to birth beneath
The promise of a rainbow.
It pauses, an oblation eclipsing evil,
Beauty lodging in a silhouette of holiness.

99 My Holy King

A song serves the Lord poor, its chants tarnish.
Its signs cross no limits, falter before keys
And times, can never sing majesty, holiness;
Can never translate continuities of
Your love celebrated in this temple.

Feeble tensions of sound in my song
Cannot scale your desires
Or boast your power to divide nations,
Subdue their anger and riot, and
Teach barbarity necessities of justice.

The resonance of song, new landscapes
Of pitch and tone, ancient voices of
Priests and prophets calling, cannot
Accent and arrange analogy to discover you.
Only love shapes love.

100 My Joy

My voice aches for the
Still sound of this Lord.
My song's surge – from dullness
And dubiety – is to suns of joy.

Hear earth's sound
Distil to *halleluia.* He moulds
Congruence from diversity,
Dawn from new-laid fires of light.

Join creation's rejoicing for
In black bud: blossom;
In the down-rush: rising;
In anguish: a child.

Joy! Scan it. It is
Fragments: complete again;
Wrongs: ravished in forgiveness;
Heartbreak: healed in love.

101 My Way

My song quarries too deep for words
To say, *I serve*. Lord,
Teach my service to raise
Again ancient purity
Within my people,
To root the untimed in time.

I will walk the ways you mark
Towards justice
And a levelling freedom;
Towards a peace
To quieten cursing
And subdue the night.

My way is not to those –
Dense with lies –
Who banish parity,
Exchange love
For convention,
And drain truth to custom.

It is with those whose wisdom
Is duty and mercy,
Whose experience
Is forgiveness,
And whose morality
Is your love.

My pain – fury trapped in
Weakness – seeks witness
For its blind scream.
Do not pass without notice
For I am yours, Lord.

Always alone – agony patents
My life – and no man's guest,
An absurd icon of your love,
I have received this
Inheritance: men's hate.

A lost son – refused redress
Daily – harried by death, I am
Neither intact nor defined,
But soon a dead mouth
Will make no complaint.

Can this night bring song?
Could glory be reborn?
Beauty is my obsession, but
Will it delight my life again
Or must I dream? Dream ...   ...

Petitions end, words are mint,
Exiles return to their lodges,
Causes set aside are heard,
The broken are mended and
Earthly wishes are heaven-granted.

The vision goes.
Time wastes my strength,
Light is bleak, pain turns back
And death waits.
The word beneath words flees.

103 God Is Love

My joy is silent adoration,
For there is no agreement
Between words and passion here.

Only a lexicon of stillness blesses,
Compresses the simplicity of love,
Translates the emptiness God. It recalls:

The crook of arms stretched to rescue,
Pardoning words importing mercy,
Hands cupped to cure.

Love, prior to time – not then, not now;
Prior to place – not here, not there;
Inarticulate, reaches for us.

You stain our ways with wet clay
And hedge flowers, write
Inaudible music for rocks and earth.

You care for us, our children,
And draw your holy image in us
As we wrestle in quiet to adore you.

Life – a summer lightning – is swiftly dumb,
Flickers sharply till played out,
Till snapping death takes our striving.

But you do not forget us.
You gather us for a homecoming:
At which love serves us.

Within nothing – black, sheer, deeper than night,
Beyond light, with no height or measure, further than space –
Hope implodes to establish an exclave.

A primordial making shapes earth and confining seas,
A ravenous vacuum spins out winds and skies,
Mediating clouds lay deep-fresh ferns.

You single out for delight gulls that skim and skate
At a tide's edge, barley in the lea fields, reeds
That pipe a descant to the sing of sanderlings.

Cow parsley crowding lanes, hanging dew in torn flowers,
Spring's plenitude, instalments of nature – fecund
Conjectures – astonish, daze us to stillness.

Your touch disturbs the subsoil, your gloss drenches
Pomegranate seeds, spring earth, oats and beans.
Your shine is in morning bread and settling wine.

You hollow out brown deserts, touch meadow orchids,
Know the green awakening of sorrel, peas and
Flowered nettles – mysteries of love's creation.

Gales scour off withered leaves, ocean shells
Lisp strange chants, repeating the waves' lament for
A sea's dead. We commend yours to you in tiny prayers.   . . .

Here, in this matted sedge and further than Orion
Or Scorpius, in all that's done, is the pulse of light,
A promise that last year's butterflies will fly again.

You stipple us – and all children – with your image.
Now things remembered do not die but are mended
Mint through the agony of your renewing love.

Swaddled in mystery, saying a word older than stars,
You – dramatist of the incongruous – forge, from ancient
Fire, symbols and language to stir your glory: in us, for us.

105 Hope and Promise

Celebrate! Sing God's psalm, for his shadow waits in
Our story – an incoherent song, an adversity encased
In the asymmetry of history.

Our vigil is a long night, shadow night, with a beginning
Foretold before any beginning. Dark-lit ancestors thought
A promise – God's promise – and wandered spare plains to seize it.

It led them – unfulfilled and dry – to an alien land, full and
Flooding, where they risked the future in a forgetful exile
Of prosperity, in a banishment of rich slavery.

The promise brought an inventory of punishments from
Those outside reason's force, scoring backs and minds.
But it anointed them with an energy of will: hope.

For this they gave up gain, were new-born from death;
For this they consented, were betrothed in desert wastes;
And found the ancient promise of love in scratching sand.

The promise took them, sifted, torn, past old
Boundaries to green uplands and new intuition,
To fresh light filtrating mysterious echoes.

They flirted with other icons and loose fancies,
But through mercy this past died to present forgiveness.
So the promise was passed to us.

Celebrate! Now in a landscape of lowly men and women
The promise overshadows; its form lies within us. With
Grave seriousness we sing its gift: love with us.

106 Forgive Disobedience

Our song is for you – though its
Scribble cannot point deep acts,
Nor give nuanced air flesh,
Nor rewrite majesty for a lower orbit.

Our canticle – pleading pardon – is
For ancestors deep-rooted in us and sin:
And us who stand with them
In its stress and consequence.

Forgive mutinous spirits untrimmed
For the wild baptism of fuming waves;
For the desert's grip, its stinging rites;
For sharp submission to your word.

Excuse dissident men honed to thin faith
Who violate prayer to patent gold;
Who abandon purity to cherish idols;
Who sully language to crush holiness.

Absolve grim men – stillborn grace –
Whose arms garner night and
Set the oblation on a tinder-tender
Altar: a child: their child, our child.

Ash on soil accuses – disobedience
Is charged to our blood.
Judge of justice, turn away. Forgiving
Father, return – though we defy love.

Our dead eyes search for you. Do not
Refuse rubrics of remembrance to us,
Else we are homeless in ourselves.
Grant your love: to beget ours.

Book
Five

107 Bless God

Together – our love, taut-tied by an
Emphatic exile – we return to this
Place, this holy space of absent song,
To sing *Halleluia* for recurrent hope.

Broken, lost on droning plains – no way-marks
Fixed – and night's terror thickly pulsing in us,
We cried in the monotony of dark. God came:
Transforming night to the first noonday sun.
Bless God for his unending gift of hope.

Lamed, pinned in crowding loneliness, trucked
To graves and torture, betraying and betrayed,
None consoling, we cried for God.
He heard, returned us – we became his again.
Bless God for his unending gift of hope.

Tangled knots of pain, choking despair, guilt –
Suppressed or denied – are difficult hurts to
Exit or excise, so we cried for God.
His salving cure discharged us, deflected death.
Bless God for his unending gift of hope.

Caught in the enmity of sea and wind –
Seamanship irrelevant, quarantined in havoc,
Safety and sense eclipsed, no lines of contact –
We cried for God: his word stilled.
Bless God for his unending gift of hope.

...

We bless him for equal love: he gives and revokes,
Speaks and is silent, shows and conceals.
We bless him for his single love: he brings fullness
To new grassland and white to the wilderness;

Judgement to princes and their people, honour to
The restrained and chaste. Always
We remember him: love bearing love.
Bless God for his unending gift of hope.

108 Come to Us

My song is learned from the sons
Of light, is rooted in a bush of fire.
A mythical word – *fiat* from the first
Air – its syntax stills to adoration.

With a reed flute it speaks of beauty:
Of dark in the light of love,
Of glory in dark spaces and stars, in
Children's delight at wet-laced webs.

You speak forgiveness to us.
In the north is my bride;
In the south my son;
In the east my daughter;
In the west my beloved.

You censure enemies with judgement.
For the north, crumbling cities, blowing dust;
For the south, barren soil, dying roots;
For the east, an exile, without return;
For the west, a wilderness, without rain.

Come to us, we are broken;
But with you we are invincible;
With you words burst their shells
And we can say again, *Our Holy One.*

109 My Innocence

From ashes my lament searches for you.
Desolation and anguish – urgent accents –
Are my necessities: for guilt of a death
Is forged against me.

Now friends are foes and hatred sits
In the habitation that was love's. Dark
Conceits, deep complicity, sworn
Lies, urge on my agony, for they say,

Let his judges unhinge justice,
Construe innocence as guilt.
Let others sing his songs and
Annex the place of his future.

Pinned to lime-washed walls in
The pit, may he and all his kin
Be burn-branded to death,
To forgetfulness.

The indifference of light lights no
Memory of him. May he hang –
Unknown, immobile, unseen –
In an emptiness without guests.

I hurt, but return their sombre curses
That confine truth, constrict my heart.
Yet now my strength – the ardour of
Morning – flies: mortality is exposed.

But, though they bury dreams of truth in
Smooth ambivalence and thin words,
You will come, winged by love, to
Heal my soul from this infinite sickness.

110 My Lord

The Lord God – source of love – speaks to
My Lord, the Son – wellspring of love – whom
I serve, and says, *Be with me. And two voices,*
An equal sonority, will make a single sound
To subdue your enemies, hold them in thrall.

Enthroned, indwelling the Lord God,
Within mutuality, you are installed:
The ineffable, a mystery – dew before
A daystar's rising. And all that is,
Is yours: what he has, you have.

The Lord God says, *You are vested – prior*
To the first heavens, before the stones,
Splintered bones, blood of ancient altars –
With glory: the scandal of forgiveness
In a loaf, in a cup.

Now, in an excess of light, you light
And finally numb the officious brutalities,
Solemnities, abstractions of unseen,
Unnamed, unnumbered shadows –
Connoisseurs in a canon of evil.

111 God

Amazed at the intimacy of grace,
Being of beings, leaven of love, we
Chant songs kindled by yearning and
Delight, for in cities, in silence, you beckon us.

Excelling all, needing none, you
Forge the fabric of circumstance to
Give to living the stain of glory,
Hint of holiness, echoes of love.

In remembrance you feed us,
Join us in joy,
Keep a continuing flame of
Love in loveless hearts.

Many gifts are given for us –
New lands, justice, peace – and
Old laws are rainbow-renewed. All
Point to, stem from, stern mercy.

Quarrying mystery, we find –
Revealed in your songs – a
Syntax of the unsayable, of
Truth: which is love.

Unapproachable yet embracing us,
Victim yet saviour,
Wrathful yet motherly,
Except we follow
You – beloved one – we are
Zeros, dust again.

Adept, the narrowed eye of the
Blessed man catches gold in
Children's eyes, wet with the
Daily threnodies of life.

Entertaining morning love, he
Finds his prayer filled and God's
Grace – improbable richness – given to
Him in dawn's gaunt grey.

Inclining a strict heart, he detects
Joy in mercy, the implication of a
Kiss – breathless compaction – and
Lives to tell of love's equality.

Many see this man's sensibility and
Name him God-haunted, herald
Of buried dreams and jimp
Pulse of past compassion.

Quick to catch each acrobatic sin, he
Rejoices with infants, with clowns, and
Sings songs of sad withdrawal with
Those who mourn in secular tongues.

Underwriting the vitality of love, the
Vicious stratigraphy of evil men is
Weighed against him. But God, who
Exacts judgement and stands with him,
Yokes them to death – these
Zealots of cant and realism.

113   A Song for You

This breath of praise is raised
To the whirlwind, to your word.
Yet its naked script – crippled
Cadence, empty image, sour
Sound – will not invade the
Privacy of your holy love.
Stripped of telling, its tactic
Is the quiet of adoration,
In which it sees this grace.

In love, you beleaguer us with
An apple-fresh summer sun,
Ripe fields where kestrels guard
Their ways; with dark honey from crushed
Berries, scents of memory, the breath and
Break of living; with joy in children
Who laugh at froghoppers,
Snailing trails, silvering bark and careless
Twists in thistles' roots.

Enthroned above cantos and
Chords of stellar sound,
From the thrum of space,
You journey to us.
You shelter here, squat here,
While we bite black bread,
Suck fish, sip blood wine
And hone wood to hold you,
To keep you in the harness of love.

114 Escape to Joy

We were defined by foes for the stress of slaves,
Given a residence of strain and shaken longing,
Our rebellion disputed their beliefs – their
Alien rites spinning nothing.

We turned away from their brutal words –
A vagrant sound of bawdy disparity,
Trivial, without beat and pitch, translating
Nothing to a vacant air.

Now, assenting captives of holiness,
We sing in the Lord's temple,
A tent through time. He hears and
Everything is returned new.

The infinite series of the sea stops;
Earth cracks, ceases its regularities;
The hills – springs of sanctuary – open;
And beasts flinch at fresh bearings.

All is teased to joy at his presence,
A nativity of light. It tips the axis
Of time to this tense: an urgency
Of love.

115 Be Our God

Our doings – time's temporary map,
Drawn with thorns and blatant
Answers – we set aside;
For glory, unnamed beauty, only
Rises deeply in your doing, Lord.

Other gods wrap vision in an
Evergreen rhetoric of gentle gossip;
Trick us to oust living for fiction;
School us in rites – stylish lies – for
Routine extinctions and deaths.

But early icons must bow to heavenly,
For you are the mastering centre –
Coming unknown to bring us home –
Around which the elisions of life,
Its intensities and conceits, pivot.

Our ancestors told us of absolutions –
Measureless stories of holy freight – and
Blessings from you. Repeat for us this
Strenuous love, the truth of things;
Image it in the crossways of our time.

I stand at midnight. Death and its implicit
Acolyte, unpaid pain, strip my life.
But the Lord stoops to hear my heart and
I am held in blinding light.

He is my host from a high air. He
Breathes the word to quicken and I am
Restored to him, to ecstasy. In sun and snow
Is our play and counter-play of love.

My thanksgiving, though mute, is known
Already – for he alone reads the rubric
Of creation, culls my span of years from
Time, records my hope in his dreams.

Yet I offer back the cup given – return love
For love – so that love's judge may drink
Fully from it and remember my people;
Breach time with eternity: and draw us home.

117 Praise

This word – a song's excess – meshes
Patterns of hope, seeks to
Inscribe from a grammar of glory,
Translate sounds to praise.

It is a simple song of the Lord's love
For his peoples – he knows their
Plight and hears their pleas; for all that
Is, he paints in rejoicing colours of life.

Praise him for his faithfulness to us,
Which hides an innerness of pain.
Praise him for his mercy, which is
The antechamber to his love.

118 A Liturgy of Gratitude for Faith

Compelled by the consequences of love –
Drawn by the urgencies of mercy,
Favours of the beloved –
Each choir's testimony, king's, priests',
People's, is to the plenitude of grace.

And my song is a mimesis of theirs.
For, when in tumult – late frosts clawing
Spring's blossom to earth – I edged to
Endorse death, a barque brought you
To the reaches of my heart.

When bleached pastures blazed,
Smoke choked and light was veiled;
When traps tightened and plans were put,
You saw my foes – locusts from a ceaseless sky –
And came to me: you whom none overcome.

The promise of friends had failed.
Their denials – facile words refracting
Pain – unmasked night.
Then you took my life – banned, dismal –
And made it the capstone of this temple.

Festal doors swing open for thanksgiving.
Steadfast prayer welcomes; the Lord's beloved
Ascends to the altar of sacrifice.
Choirs sing this joyous anthem of praise.
Blessed are you in your house, great God, our Father.

119 Aphorisms: the Law of Love

Ah, rejoice with those whose feet are fleet for love,
  who dance with moon moths and morning stars.
Bless them, for they tread a way twinned to glory
  through crowded summer reeds and stiff grey gorse.
Compelled by the sovereignty of longing, they drag
  dark and comb light to reach, touch, your feet.
Draw them to you, bodies of dust, drained of greenness,
  dry; delight them with unchecked life, your deepest gift.

Etch your words on my heart, press your hand to mine,
  import the currency of obedience – a slow exchange.
Fill cupped hands with your mercies – memoration
  of stern oblations and flying forgiveness.
Give strength that, in a night of exile, I may not
  halt the remembrance of you, stay your grace.
Hour to hour, courteous love's landscape bounds the
  tumult of life's traffic and the caprice of space.

In my house make a lodging for yourself, a tabled room;
  pots and plates for love to celebrate its service, equality.
Judge me; join me to the community of those who drum
  doors to decipher mute stones and see unseen sufferings.
Know me as one who waits – segmented seasons, vexed
  hours, unsettling days – for the opportunity of eternity.
Lord, I love the law of love, reticulation of awesome beauty;
  bind me to its unbearable prescription, ardent provocation.

May my way mirror your way, know you in city streets,
a damselfly's meadow flight and the ecumenism of truth.
No light than yours will light the freedom-fire of the future,
the intimacy of word and creation, the inner necessity of
love.
Only you can sustain me against enemies, expel negation,
arrest antagonism, marshal a sun for the rites of bliss.
Pledge yourself to me – pining in winter's thin days for
you – as custodian of joys, precisian of love's grammar.

Quietly, you examine the analogies of my life – tired
postulates, unverified expectancies – and
Raise me to a persuasive reality, the idiom of
holiness, a daring context for dancing love.
So, when despised and sorrowing, trapped in endemic
evil and irritant unbelief, targeted by pain, I turn to you.
The loveliness of your presence – in sifted lives, split
stones on frozen turf, wrinkled skin – is an
Unsolved answer to ill-fitting fragments dismissed
in daily prayers.

Voices close, words stop, the vigil ends. I notice you
just past the strand lines of stillness,
Waiting, reminding me whose I am, laughing at my
discontent with arbitrary and approximate days.
Excellent Lord – of sycamore seeds and my children,
of life's hope and death's health –
Your love, an unforced but exact focus, shows what
cannot be seen – and each glance deepens mystery.
Zeal for you, life from you, joyously turn each day:
may they still thrill when dark and final dances draw me.

120 Threats Against Me

I looked for peace and found war;
I journeyed for love and received hurt.
Accused by anonymous breath at night,
Its lies rebuked, bred confusion
And imprisoned my spirit.

I crossed mountains betrothed to clouds;
I wandered cities that blasphemed green plains.
Always deceit caught me, unseen voices
Put false charges. I fear the spite of men,
But more the mendacity of human hearts.

Without your strength, I fail. Protect me.
Bring to those who set their tongues
And tortures against me, your judgement.
For, when I seek peace, they pursue war;
When I give love, they whisper, *Betray*.

121 My Protector

I seek silences which assemble in high ranges,
Collect in the vacancy of remote plains,
Inhabit the interludes of prayer:
For these are homes the Lord loves.

From them – setting aside the
Mosaic of stars and spun threads
For spiders' webs – he comes,
Cloaked in the strangeness of time.

He protects me from annulment in exile
And the ingenuities of venal years;
From the density of familiar and daily evil;
From the hurt of sensuality – grey,

Corrosive, monotonous – from which love
Has withdrawn. He protects me when,
Choked by the manners of neighbours,
I retreat from freedom.

He protects for himself, for my joy.
In a rapture of quiet, I adore.
Drawn to closeness, the delicate exchange
Of love is made: now sacrifice begins.

122 Jerusalem

My heart leaps – spring's driven
Blossom quivers in delight –
When, flooded by longing and
Prayers from the night,
It hears the chant for Jerusalem.

Let us adore the beloved, her heart.
May peace – measure of love – circle her homes;
May peace – enclosure of love – live within her;
May peace – fruit of love – be hers everlastingly,
Citadel of joy and judgement, hope and healing.

Drawn by her beauty – hatched in the
Lord's care – and rose-shadowed towers,
We stood in the courts of Jerusalem
To hear the index of salvation. Forever
Now, each journey journeys to her, to him.

123 We Wait

As suppliants,
In watchful alertness – a concise ear poised,
Eyes pursuing eyes – for the Lord to turn
His face, we wait.

As captives –
Shrouded in winter's fear, our hope lynched –
With no promise of restoration, for the
Loving-pity of the Lord, we wait.

As slaves,
Whose names – registered pariahs, listed to receive
Contempt – are forfeit till a time of
Redemption, we wait.

124 The Saviour

When the flood breaks and deeps foam,
Rushing us to the inconsequence of death;
When there is no path but pain – shards
Shaping the way – and scorpions spike our feet;
When we are adorned in brown blood and
Nakedness for the mouth of the abyss;
Then, without your holiness,
We are powerless.

When stalking wolves run and
Leopards strain to leap;
When carrion crows come to
Tear our cheeks and flies hiss;
When the seat of death is on our face, you
Run to us – forgotten lives – to still our fear;
And anoint us:
A people for the Lord.

125 God's Bride

Jerusalem, a bride, waits for her Lord;
Stillness magnifies her beauty.
A great city, set on silent mountains –
His mountains, holy mountains,
Glory-crowned mountains – for peace,
She calls to him.
Faith is her perilous song.

The Lord will unite with her loveliness,
Protect her from all who itch for evil
And license chaos.
A rest for the harried and uncertain,
She stoops to kiss the feet of those who –
Crossed with pain and truth – walk in
Purging flames for love's future.

Then
No longer did night's black subdue us
    to unfamiliar horizons;
No longer did death's chill tune us
    to self-doubt and silent torment;
No longer did the east wind shrive
    our bones and shrivel hope;
No longer did our sadness solicit
    canonical laments;
For the panic of undoing was undone
    and dreams we used to know fulfilled.
Even the nations – cautious, waiting for
    deceit – saw it and were amazed,
And laughed with us at children playing
    their perennial games of *catch* and *chase*.

But soon holy gifts were turned away.

Now
May they return to us. Imbue our land with
    your design, intent;
Refresh us with barley, rice and butter-milk,
    sweet chestnuts and lemon mint;
Gladden us with springs and rivers, new water
    from wells, wine from evening bowls;
Father here wild marjoram, silky eels,
    buckeye butterflies, and determined wasps.
Feed us: as there is earthly meat, may there
    be heavenly bread.
Give us name and purpose again, pledge prosperity
    and a warming sun.
Then this: grant that we – awkward and
    inconsequent – may catch epiphanies of love.

127 All Is the Lord's

Though we call to those without sight for insight,
Tax words – infirm, arbitrary – for meanings;
Though we seek hope in lingering dreams of prophets,
Build faith – seasoned innocence – from charged living;
All we propose arises from you.

The form of cities, the music of songs,
The wit of wisdom, the play of paint;
Inward possibility – beyond conscious
Command – or outward articulation;
Nothing we purpose arrests your resolve.

All is imbued with glory,
Figured and formed by your will.
Aldebaran and Ursa, comfrey and squill,
Babies who cry, infants who crawl,
Sons and daughters: all sing your love.

As life slips out – many seasons,
Many dreams – and I crop
Neither shadows nor light,
I know that, with his dearest love,
The Lord has loved me dearly.

My bride – and her song, impulse
Of language for the speech of Eden –
Was his love's gift. And veiled in
Wonder and the screening darkness, he
Grafted joy to our lives.

Our children – apricot-fresh and rosy,
Laughter in the morning rise, moulded
To make the potter sigh a smile –
Gave a deeper seeing. Unknowing, they
Foretold fluent oaths and the play of eternity.

129 My Enemies

A quarry from birth, racked by
Foes – friends of worsted gods –
Who stalk time to splinter sense,
My end falls: and silence.

Harried by the authority of inhumanity –
A mutiny, unspeakable confrontation,
Unbearable imagining – and terror,
My end falls: and silence.

Yet God eclipses their night with sun,
Seizes their crests for children's games,
Mocks provocations and self-flattery,
Before my end falls: in silence.

He rewards my foes' feverish indifference
With a prosperity of thin seed and barren soil.
With love's festal word, he blesses us and
We fall to this end: silent adoration of him.

130 My Agony

No sound inhabits this empty place.
But ice-white torment shivers sinews,
Shakes me endlessly; always
The imperative of guilt and
Its staining pain.

Nothing is housed in this vacancy
But sucking dust and waiting – and
Awkward cross-echoes of my
Trespass. Grace-filled Lord,
Hear me, forgive.

Censored within round-round
Walls of self-hatred, for sin
I dare not disown, I hear
The interdiction. But Lord,
Have mercy, forgive.

As a summer maiden, at the gate
Of the apple orchard, waits
For love, peers into a morning mist;
So, a snared soul watches
For forgiveness, mercy.

From a maze of lies, your
Love – truth wed to suffering,
Faith born to hope, locking
Arms of grace – draws me, renews;
Kisses apple cheeks again.

131 Contemplation

I sit simply in your story – forgoing
Self-assertion, seeking no contention –
To learn its haunting moods, its deep sadness
And its infinite life.

I attend quietly to your paradoxes –
Shunning licensed power, pomp and
Dashing ascendancy – to understand
The domesticity of your love.

I gaze long to your beauty – forgetting
Eminent rivalries and the apparel
Of pride – and look, child-like, into
Your eyes holding all eyes.

As a child for her mother, I sing
Songs for you, joys whose
Form is prayer, chants breaking:
The finality of death.

In this high hour, words migrate
To silence, gladness outruns our tongues;
In this high place, frontiers are breached,
And life's loaded dreams fashion truth.
For a shepherd king remembers
His ancient vow to the Lord.

A nomad across desert-days
And constellations of the night,
I will not regard my ease, ease my
Prayer, until a place for your
Rest — cosmic solitude — is
Gauged among these discursive hills.

From nonsense rhymed by shepherd lads
To laugh away summer's days, to the
Severe lament of frosted winter's time,
Our songs urged your ark to this city.
Its altar, a fit harbour for your
Unceasing presence.

Now your promise is unveiled;
Its prophecy, placed in truth's strict syllables,
Says this. *My love — tutelary, sovereign,*
Unageing — is invested in your kings.
It remains in this place, this cradle
Of grace for suffering, of holiness.

Now you come to stay, stay to bless, us
And all life: midday midges and hedge
Lilies, foreign cloud, and corn and hay.
You nerve us to follow beauty's arc,
Watch a love — tight-stretched,
Upright in sunshine — for us.

133 Unity

There is joy in concord for all people
When words say new what is seen fresh;
When voices sing songs to mend broken speech
And make sound whole;
When fragments, indifferent and abandoned,
Make an unheard harmony.

There is blessing in concord for all people when
The Lord anoints his high priest –
Counterpoint to holiness – with love.
He kneels, his prayers inflect
Supplications with freedom:
With suffering.

There is peace in concord for all people
When bread is shared, beggars embrace,
Donors repent and healing abounds.
For unity is a story attuned – in
Mysterious triple echoes – to
Love's glory.

To be, and to be in this place of holiness,
Is to be touched with radiance and a
Silence numbing thought.
We tremble for the stillness is
A packed possibility, is love's prologue.

At this astonishment in prayer
We speak blessings – from an
Inventory of rough words, pecked, imperfect,
Buffeted by use, cramped, and child-stamped –
For you.

Then new words – words new-forged,
Fresh as winter air and yellow aconites,
Gleaming as wedding wine, beaming as
New-baked bread, intent as infants' eyes –
Travel to us: your smiling blessings.

135 Praise and Praise Again

New praise at dawn is our delight.

Praise the Lord in his temple, a villa
Not harnessed by time or the gravity of space.
Defying thought and deftness in logic, he is –
Moulded to beauty's form – when we are not.

Praise the Lord, who swifts with
Swallows and wind-winged clouds;
Smiles as butterflies flatter may-blossom
And frosts kiss a white winter's moon.

Praise the Lord, who tenants justice,
Encircles his people. From an exile of pain
By wordless rivers and stinging air, he called us
To a desert, to a servitude of freedom.

Praise the Lord, who masters fury in his enemies.
Death leered – when they, jealous rivals, averred
Primacy over him – to take them. He marked
Their lands, a bequest, a future for us, his beloved.

Praise the Lord who – discarding the syntax of
Usage and convention, bending language
Beyond rule-bound frontiers – speaks to bless:
Let love for all be all-given.

New praise at dawn is our delight.

136 Love Everlasting

The Lord's love is an everlasting love.
In unfathomable immensities, he places
The fervour of space and spinning fire,
The swing of light and ripening nova,
The urgent traffic of Pisces and Pyxis.
As is the eye of love, creation is
Porous to his glory.

The Lord's love is an everlasting love.
He elected an arduous, severe people,
Incited their – indefensible – hope,
Prescribed the sea's limit, drew a path
To the secret discipline of love.
As is the eye of the just, history is
Porous his glory.

The Lord's love is an everlasting love.
He halted lucubrations of barbarism, put
Foes to silence, brought friends to new lands,
Appointed them exegetes of hope,
A place for its birth, a nativity of light.
As is the eye of the prophet, the future is
Porous to his glory.

The Lord's love is an everlasting love.
He absolves anathemas, gives mercy to life,
Gathers bread scattered to the mountains,
Draws wine blazed by the sun, in joy –
Crossed with agony – feeds his people.
His eyes refract glory for their eyes. Seeking,
They learn to speak the first speech: his speech.

137 Silent Mourning

In a dry of monotonous plains,
By a series of silent canals,
Under shades of still willows,
We interpose tears.

Narrows of thought, sanded
Deep, give words no home to
Shape songs for foes – nor mould
Music, to echo their tropes of joy.

Our repertoire slides to grief,
Contiguities have fled. Beauty is
Fettered. We learn tempers of despair
And linger with remembrance.

Exile without hope, loss without
Return, suffering without check,
Exodus without freedom, speech
Without promise: we are smitten.

Though shrunk to slavery, we are
Rapt by Jerusalem – rounded in hope.
Cursed be those who implant a canon
Of inhumanity in children's hearts.

This temple promotes in my thoughts –
Hidden dreams, immature hopes –
A pulse of thanksgiving; gratitude for the
Canniness inhabiting ordinary parts.

Cancelling distinctions and separation,
You return the familiar to an unfamiliar.
Night blurs the almond trees and
Slow fog twists down mountain tracks.

The sun's haze paints new pale puffballs
And blue chicory. The ebbing tide recedes
To another shore – and the haven is always
Heaven. So I sing ungrudging thanks

For you came to my side when I cried;
Freed me from foes; exalted the modest,
Plain, restrained; and toppled those
Whose thoughts circled about themselves.

Ever my thanks for your mystery, refracted in
Unacknowledged lives and a damp dog rose;
In truth, which always catches to surprise;
In me who find you, the beloved: in love's wounds.

139 The Beloved's Love

Within the shy touch of your perplexing love,
I know I am known, closely purposed.
Within the first *fiat*, a matrix of being,
You created, not with an abstract eye in
Loneliness but with fingers of intractable love,
Inventing destiny and yearning, tongue and toes.

You see my way on homeless roads, unsettled seas,
Unresting waits in trackless wastes, and mark them.
Yet there is only beginning, ever only beginning –
And eternity is taxed to begin all beginnings – for
You are God whose beginning is without end: and
My end is a beginning in love, renewed without end.

If, when seas are full above, I follow avenues
Stamped by Behemoth, and hide in caves of gloom
Where all paths cease; if, through raging suns,
I fly down labyrinths of space, evade light, dark,
And seal myself in sadness, silence; you do not
Forget – you founded my spirit – but seek me,

Address, caress, all to complete me.
Then I, wounded, return to you and you,
Wounded by me, ring me round with mercy.
Racing to an infinite edge, we pause at the
Perimeter of love and I know bliss; the shepherd
Of being – mysterious mutuality – breathes in me.

140 Rescue Me, Lord

Dry tears can tear a heart and blood pulse cold.
The words of enemies – observing precise
Conventions of slander – scar the past,
Betray my present, extinguish future hope.

A cipher, I founder in their imposing savagery and
Ungoverned hate. In this landscape – the province
For such loathing is the charnel vault – of serial
Insensibility, there can be no words, no saying.

There is not a tongue to master this suffering
To speech or form: ashes breed no songs.
Thought is impotent and spirit split.
There's no music in terror: suns are fractured.

Without antidotes for barbarism I call to God,
To unlimited love. His words – truth without
Metaphor – are not veiled. He sees my foes'
Evil, archaic efficiency and ruthless indifference.

Sin's prime translators, they revise texts daily, adapt
Incantations, solicit sequels. But the severe reproof
Of love – a spinning rose of fire – unhinges time and
They move to a dark drawn by their own sins.

141 Temptation

As the sun gathers up its final light,
Lovers wait for the night's dark,
Priests for the evening star, and
I attend to prayer for your presence.
Eyes live. Behold, I am beheld: and fear.

Temptation — a hungry tabulation of
Passion and control — escalates to
Feigned truth, disproves innocence,
Divides desire from will and
Draws me to its exquisite brink.

Turn me from this brutality which
Binds my spirit to ambition, yokes
Me to a treadmill of rounding fantasies.
Tune me fully to your severe mercy,
A discipline of suffering love.

Teach me to frame the form of psalms,
To line my days with mystery,
To seek epiphanies of glory — among
Unsorted stars, muttering ducks — and
Receive the dearest gift of grace: you for me.

Despair is my only tone.
My spirit is dismembered.
My tongue has no speech.
Only my heart calls.

Continuities of life –
Flower-time, fruit-time –
Fall. There is no outside:
For this is the hour ending hours.

My dungeon silence –
No willow warblers,
Screaming gulls – detects
Other silences.

The stillness of those
Who know – but say not;
The quiet complicity of foes;
A voiceless impotence of friends.

Lord, my empty breath recalls:
None so stay as you. Raise me
That I may be rightly me.
Bless being. May the sun rise.

143 My Dungeon

Anger warps light, twists the talk
Of serious foes, stretches my anguish.
Evil's fevered colours mask their faces;
Lies officiate at this trial to steal my life.

I am hounded to concealed dungeons,
Where the stings of fire fire my fears
And light burns; where I pray for rain
And receive incense of burning blood.

Naked and white, in ante-chambers of night,
I listen for your peculiar song – a soundless
Music – of close love. With expectant eyes
I look for dawn, a further day: and wait.

Come, before I am unable to begin again,
Before alternatives fade and cycles cease;
Before I am cracked open and
Emptied in a wink of eternal darkness.

Free my spirit – wing-pinned butterfly –
Abandoned, snapped, gilded with tears.
Turn my exile – crushed ash – to noon's song,
For you are all the love my heart can breed.

144 Victory

I touch your love – unshuttered possibility –
In storm and peril, while rituals of pain
And prayer hollow out my life. You remain
With me through needless deaths, weeping.

The recurrent ring of your word is wed
To my cross-grained doubt. I shelter
Under a bridal sun, for this little life-night
Is a shadow from holy light.

My new songs – scavenging transcriptions,
Scrawls from the vast utterance of glory –
Sing of your victory against the menace,
Deadening babel, of howling enemies.

Lord, your gifts – you father rain and
Free soil, shape form and give substance,
Set hope to belief and replenish all at your
Table – to us, define your heart: love.

145 God - an Alphabet of Praise

All names are yours, Lord: but who are you?
Beauty and hiddenness. A king enthroned. You
Crown creation: a charcoal fire, fish, bread.
Dancing, we celebrate your power. It sustains
Each day, each life, each world, all being.
Freshness too – frosted fields, rouged blossom,
Green leaves teasing breezes – is a music of
Heaven's hue and echoes silent praise.
I know your grace: a majesty where gladness is
Joined to justice and patience to peace.
Keep me in remembrance of your glory;
Let all people see it, wonder at your pity and
Mercy, a living bread for all. You make
New: corrupt, awry and sin-set times.
Opening loving arms – wider than death – you
Proclaim forgiveness for our guilt, embrace us,
Quieten fear. You stay with us, stoop to
Rescue us. We are caught in death's snares,
Set – a brutality of nuanced precision – by
Those who hate us. Confer grace upon
Us, offer the cup of joy, lift our eyes to the
Vision of your holiness. Then
We, in the gift – everlasting sacrifice,
Extraordinary oblation – of
Your love, share love and becomes its
Zealous and continuing disciples.

146 Rejoicing in God

My heart's pull of love solemnises
Language, and my song – interleaving
Tensed awe and dense thought –
Seeks the nerve of glory.

Fidelity sanctifies prayer and I look
Only to you. For though men's dreams
Map powers and times, their season is brief;
Scenes end and shadows strut the dark.

You turn to me and I hear your promise
Of freedom and suffering;
It lives in me and I in it, for you
Are my beloved, my delight.

You are love let loose.
You touch our lives – turned aside –
To clothe and feed us, to care
And heal us, to save and free us.

So my heart initiates this chant – the
Innermost heart of whose words is your
Word – of praise. *You are beauty of all
Beauty, hope of all hope, till time is timed away.*

147 Jerusalem Rebuilt

Glory garners children's words –
Playful metrics, simple songs –
For the reaches of risen joy.

The Lord's lost are home-called,
Sad exiles are heart-mended,
Gathered to his side, his city.

He, who gave fledglings flight,
Snow's bright and roses' fire,
Has healed our ancient wound.

We feared – harried by inhumanity,
Novelties of barbarity – but he
Crowned weakness with love.

White walls sang, gates shouted, Glory.
Children were blessed and we rejoiced;
Peace walked in our ways.

The Lord gives bread for our need,
Wine in our want; brings forgiveness
And rejoicing to the feast.

Torn garments are mended,
Walls stretched straight again,
A widow is bride.

148 A Song of Cosmic Praise

To praise this God seek the deep grammar of halleluia;
Speak free of speech and shape fresh psalms.
Evoke from Babel – riven plurality – a new-shaped
Syntax to whisper awe anew at gifts of love. Stammer
Mysterious meanings.

What is dances with his word and sings for him:
The deeps of dark light-time; ice-ringed suns;
White anemones; new-born freshness; windfall frosts.

What is dances with his word and sings for him:
Stars in spate; coiling gases, orange and purple,
Gold and green; immigrant terns and racing hares.

What is dances with his word and sings for him:
Whales processing anonymous oceans; quibbling
Rooks, and butterflies flirting in the cense of red lilies.

What is dances with his word and sings for him:
Linden trees, lemon and quince, and yellow suns
Of sunflowers; the bewilderment of seasons passing.   ...

What is dances with his word and sings for him:
Priests with broken-back prayers; unsettled rulers,
Cautious dramatists of delay; and run-racing children.

What is dances with his word and sings for him:
All that is chosen to be in creation's burst; all who
Dream in starfields and wait for an ancient crib.

Such a halleluia – outrunning reason's lexicon –
Will invest embossed language with warmth and
Sense; will mould again words heavy with age –
Thick words, imperfect words – and unfurl a
Vocabulary to plead absence present.

149 His People Rejoice

Incited to joy by your gifts of love,
Our song – an unequal counterpoint to
Glory – is heard in the summer of time as
Storm birds rest, and clouds neatly skim the sea.

This temple chant – mysterious pathology
Of language – fuses awe with delight;
Makes thanksgivings for our king, for
He moulds us to the fate of freedom.

Transposing sound to the ambition of
Limbs – a subtle paraphrase – we
Dance, for holiness flares flame, enemies
Recede, victory clenches each fist.

Set our imprecise praise – filtered
Through glory's fine fire – to
The tensions of pity and mercy,
The supple styles of peace.

150 Praise, Simply Praise

Adoration is the single impulse of my heart.
Crowding words query grammars of glory
To sift new shapes for praise.
The bewilderment of languages speaks this –
Eden's only word – *Halleluia, Halleluia.*

The hinge of space is raised: awesome
Horizons, an energy of colour. Light and
Dark, eager to exalt the meaning set in the
Silence at the centre of things – alien deeps,
Starbursts at the Southern Cross – give praise.

Creation's song – of what is new-found in
Old seeing, new-born from vacancy or
New-given in grace – solicits praise from each
Season's slow axis: hale hollyhocks, roses'
Spice, berries' blood, sour vinegar, still wood.

The sound in things – all babbling and rending;
The vibrancy of being – in crows and coyotes;
All that sings – cymbals, bells, drums and shells:
Are tuned to joy, to the register of praise.
All that is, that breathes, sings: *Halleluia, Halleluia.*